To see what all the fuss is about, read on...
...and to receieve new Journals as they're published, visit:
daily.stuartcarter.co.uk

Anthology, Vol.1

Bite-Sized Nuggets of Simplicity and Clarity for Busy Business Owners

Stuart Carter

I am deeply grateful to those without whom life would be more complicated than it needs to be...

Tracy Prentice *for supporting me hugely over the summer of 2017 while I encountered the most bewildering time of my life to date.*

Michelle Powis *for making Yoga accessible to this inflexible, overweight newbie.*

Carl Edwards *for being Carl. Always positive, always enthusiastic, and taught me how to leave inhibitions on the side and enjoy a boogie!*

Jason Leister *for being a unique, inspiring voice at a time when I thought the whole world might be fake.*

My wonderful **Master Minders** *for their unwavering awesomeness.*

And, as always, the wonderful **Helen,** *my wife, who is* still *patiently putting up with my constant philosophical ramblings!*

—

Thank-you all.

—

Disclaimer

The contents of this book do not constitute individual advice to the reader. The ideas, procedures and suggestions contained in this book are not intended as a substitute for consulting with a professional business adviser. Neither the author nor the publisher shall be held liable or responsible for any loss or damage allegedly arising from any information or suggestion in this book.

Introduction

"Oh god! What have I just done?"

I'd just made a commitment to my coach (yes, coaches have coaches too!) I'd committed to writing a daily journal entry and publishing into the big wide world for anyone who would care to read it.

Up to this point I'd had trouble even writing one blog per month.

I'd previously been hiding behind a mask of perfection; keeping my light hidden in case anyone saw it and called me out on my flaws. People might disagree with me, or quietly mock me. People might think that what I'm writing is 'micky mouse' stuff that *everyone* knows.

Oh, how *vulnerable* I was going to make myself if I wrote something—whatever was on my mind—each day...

But the commitment was made, so I decided to *speak my truth*. I decided to write, each day, something that I think might help others. Simple as that.

It's not all 'original thought' (what is?), but you can guarantee that everything I've written been filtered through my 'being'. I don't regurgitate wisdom, I *live it* and then pass on those parts that I think are most helpful, in the way that I think is most accessible.

I write this journal as a reminder for myself as much as to help others, and putting this anthology together has reminded me of many things I may have let slip since first talking about them.

I'll be dipping into my own copy over time, letting chance decide what lesson I could learn today, and I hope that's one way *you,* too, might choose to ingest the nuggets from between these pages.

Or go cover-to-cover if you wish, but I'd implore you *not to race.* Don't just read each entry, say to yourself "that's nice" and move on. This is a work for savouring. Take each nugget like a fine food... bite it off, chew it thoroughly, enjoy the flavour and give it time to digest. This way you won't only feed the conscious mind, but you'll also nourish your subsconscious.

However you choose to read this book, I hope you find it helpful and if you'd like more of the same—and you're not already subscribed to my 'Journal to Your Inbox'—you can join us here:

http://daily.stuartcarter.co.uk

It has truly been a joy to provide my journal to the world since March 2017, and I will continue through 2018 and beyond.

I wish you all the best in your business and your life, and please get in touch if you would like to discuss anything further. If you have questions, comments, or you just plain disagree with something, do drop me an email. I don't promise to reply quickly, but I will do my very best to respond to everyone who takes the time to write...

Now dive in! Enjoy!

Stuart Carter
January 2018
stuart@stuartcarter.co.uk

The Journals, 2017

1 If it doesn't happen, it might just not be for you

I think back to the number of times I've kind-of wanted to do something, or thought I *should,* and when expected to follow through it just hasn't happened.

And for the most part, there was a good reason for my resistance. It wasn't the *right thing to do.* My gut feel used every obstacle in its power to prevent me from taking action, whatever my 'thinking brain' told it.

But likewise, when I've committed to doing something important; whatever the odds, however many the naysayers, I've *always* achieved it. Even when the task would seemingly need divine intervention—or a lot of luck at the very least—to achieve.

And so the question is...

Am I putting this off due to fear? Due to being too 'small'? Or is it actually just *not for me right now?*

When it is, you'll know it.

2 The desire to hit the target

As an aspiring archer who also speaks Japanese, I've been interested to learn about *Kyūdō* recently. It's the Japanese 'martial art' form of archery.

And it turns out that in order to excel in *Kyūdō*, one must have a completely clear mind when executing one's shot.

In fact, at high-level competitions, points are deducted if it's thought that the archer has too much desire to hit the target.

The same can be said in business. When we focus on the target—when we get attached to the outcomes—we get tense and anxious and we no longer do our best.

We are aiming simply to *be our best self* and *do our best work*, and the targets will take care of themselves.

3 Done is better than perfect

I know. Guilty as charged.

I get so hung up on perfection. On dotting every t, and crossing every i. (Or something like that, yes?)

But sometimes, we've just got to get the thing out there. It has more value by being out there in an imperfect form, than filed away on a to-do list to put those finishing touches on.

Done is better than perfect.

(That's not to say we should be putting total cr!p out there... as my Platinum Master Minders often remind one another... "Good is good enough. But sh#t isn't.")

4 The "Stunt Watch"

I'm quite ascetic really. I don't put much value on big houses, fancy cars or any of that jazz. (In my opinon, there are much better places to put my money; and if you've read The Millionaire Masterplan[1], or otherwise have a 'wealth mindset' you might agree!)

Anyway... watches are probably the one thing I really like. I could spend some crazy money on them if I wasn't careful. Like 'small investment property in the North of England' money.

But I don't.

I have a nice enough watch. It's smart, simple and does the job.

But I also like walking. And that tends to involve tree branches, rocks and sweat.

So thus far I've been unaware of the time while walking, which is no bad thing.

---

1. The Millionaire Masterplan, Roger James Hamilton, ISBN: 978-1455583997

But I thought I'd get myself a "stunt watch". You know, something cheap and replaceable. Something with a webbing strap. Something that's nicely water resistant for the inevitable "liquid sunshine" that Britain so abundantly provides us with.

But it bugs me.

You know I'm a recovering perfectionist, yes?

Well, the second hand ticks *between* the marks.

Ouch!

I'm tempted to buy a watchmaking kit, pull it apart and set it right.

But then I remember. It's cheap. And it's imperfect. And in that imperfection is a kind of beauty. And a lesson.

It does the job, and it does it admirably. The second hand landing right *on* the marks is just not important.

And I guess we should remember that in our day-to-day life and business. Remember what's important, and what just isn't.

And when it comes down to it, most of it isn't.

5 The 'shoddy draft'

A few days ago I talked about "done is better than perfect."

And something came up in my Platinum Master Mind today... one of the members posted his "shoddy draft" of a video.

I suddenly realised what a magical concept this is.

Just Get The Shoddy Draft Done.

It takes almost no effort and absolutely no heartache to create a shoddy draft. Then you can either use it or refine it as you see fit.

I bet most of the time the shoddy draft will be just fine.

Stretching, or Stupid?

I love a good goal. A good challenge. Who doesn't?

But what's the nature of the goals we're looking at?

Something uninspiring doesn't call us to action. We don't have to grow; we know we can achieve a simple goal, so we don't bother.

Something impossible, likewise, doesn't inspire action. We know we have no chance of achieving the goal, so why try?

The key is to find the goal that we can *just about* scrape if we give our best.

The key is in figuring out if we've created a *stretching* challenge, or a *stupid* challenge.

And only *we* will know the answer.

7 Proof that you are not your thoughts

I've been studying mindset a lot lately, both for myself and to help clients. And I got to wondering what, exactly, is the "ego".

This is the part of us that makes us do dumb things to protect it. We don't put our best stuff out there for fear of looking silly. And if we think someone is threatening our ego, we can get quite defensive.

Eckhart Tolle (best known for writing The Power of Now[2]) puts it this way... "The ego is when you *identify* with your thoughts."

Aha. Ok... so if I think "I'm useless and can't do this.", that's fine.

If I *believe it and identify with it,* then that's the sign that my ego has taken over.

Thoughts are happening all the time. They're flying around our heads, popping up whenever they like.

---

2. The Power of Now, Eckhart Tolle, ISBN: 978-0340733509

We are *not* our thoughts.

And the proof is this:

Have you ever thought "I'm really stupid" after making a mistake?

Have you ever thought "Wow! I'm awesome!" after a success?

There's your proof.

You *can't be both.*

You are, in fact, neither. You are just *you.*

And that's the remedy to ego-thinking. Whenever you find yourself making a value judgement of yourself or others   for example "I am *always* late"—take the judgement words out of the sentence and just leave "I am."

That's all there is. You exist. You have thoughts, but you are not your thoughts. You can be anything. You can do anything.

You *are.*

A Message for the 99%

So we're not in the "one percent"?

We're the people who've missed out on the wealth? Missed out on the power? Missed out on the freedom?

There are two things that come time mind when I think of the 1% and the 99% protests.

Firstly, according to 80/20, the fact that 1% of the population holds 50% of the wealth is not unjust, it is merely a universal law. According to 80/20, twenty percent of the population will hold around eighty percent of the wealth. four percent will hold sixty-four percent, and one percent will hold half.

If you think it's unjust, go and check the peas on a pea farm. Fifty percent of the peas will be growing in one percent of the pods.

It's a natural law.

But here's the other thing, and it's far more important. It turns out that *we are in the 1%*.

You see, the problem we have is a lack of *gratitude*. We look at the 'haves' and categorise ourselves as 'have nots'.

We look at what we don't have, that we'd quite like... maybe those holidays, or the bigger house, or the 4x4...

But let's take a look at what we *do* have.

Even the poorest in the developed West have:

▶ Freedom of expression *(political, religious and idealogical)*
▶ Shelter and food.
▶ The opportunity to make money by almost any legal means.
▶ Healthcare.
▶ Transport that works, both public and private.

...and lots more besides.

Yes... we, in the developed West, are *all* the 1%.

If you'd like to see the real 99%, look at the favelas in Rio, or the slums in China, or indeed the conditions in Somalia.

9 Accurate Thought

One of the best success hacks: Accurate Thought.

Without getting emotionally entangled, without the blueprint of our upbringing or culture, without worrying what people will think of us, without kidding ourselves with either rose-tinted specs or self-told stories of doom.

Accurate Thought.

10x

10x is a big number. Imagine working with 10 times the number of clients you currently work with. Or employing 10 times the number of staff. It'll take thought, effort and risk to get there.

But there's somewhere we can all implement a 10x in our business today...

And that's in our premium pricing.

If your highest-priced product or service is not at least 10 times the price of the lowest, there's a huge chance that you're leaving money on the table.

(With enough customers, you could offer something at 100x or 1000x your base price).

But start at 10x. What can you offer? Because the money's out there with your name on it.

11 Seeing the Opportunity

I was following a property investing video today, and while I thought I was pretty good at being positive and seeing opportunities, this guy blew me out of the water.

Why?

He was talking about the new stamp duty to be paid on buy-to-let housing.

He went through the case study of a £275k property, and the fact that the stamp duty would now be over £8,000 more than before the changes.

That's enough to put you off buy-to-let, right?

Not for this guy.

The logic went thus:

Your property will most likely double in value in the next 15 years (conservatively). So will you let an £8,000 tax bill get in the way of earning £275k?

If you buy smart, your investment will bring some income, and you'll have capital gains of £18k a year on top of that.

Will you really let £8k of tax stop you doing it?

He has such a good point.

And a further point is that yes, a lot of people will let that tax bill stop them doing it. So the job for those who see the reality just got even easier.

What's the lesson here?

If an obstacle appears, many will be stopped by it. If we can see the reality and find a way around it, we're going to benefit hugely.

12 Breathe

I was working with my Young Enterprise team last week, mentoring them on their presentation skills. They ran a four-minute pitch by me, and on the first run it took four minutes and forty seconds.

We then had a small 'masterclass' and ran it through again; four minutes and *twenty* seconds.

I then had a flash of inspiration. These guys *weren't breathing.* They were getting flustered, rushing the speech.

So I made a suggestion…

"Can you do exactly what you just did, but pause and breathe."

I demonstrated.

They ran the exact same pitch again – but being conscious of their breathing. Any guesses as to the timing?

Three minutes and fifty seconds.

Sometimes we have to do things slower to fit more in. Let's be aware of our breathing, both figuratively *and* literally.

13 Responsibility

When we have an issue, we can take 100% responsibility for fixing it.

Even if it's not our fault. Even if others are involved.

Even if we think they should take responsibility – but that would require action on *their* part, and we can't bank on that.

We have to take 100% responsibility for the outcomes we want in our life. If we don't, we are at the mercy and whims of those who do.

14 "Our Idea" of Success

Wow.

I've just been through the process of looking for a new coach for myself, so had the pleasure of seeing what all the other coaches are up to right now.

And one really stood out.

It's one of those 'coaching franchise' companies. I've always been a little wary of those kind of companies, because I always wondered how their systemised coaching programme can meet their clients' *bespoke* needs.

But something worse than that came to my attention.

Their wording goes something like:

"We'll share our idea of success with you, and help you get there."

ALARM BELLS!

"Our idea of success"?

If there's anything in this world that's a personal choice, it's our own idea of success.

So these guys are saying they'll help you get the fast car and the big house, when all you wanted was a puppy.

Are people really so unimaginative that they can't even think of what success means to them?

I guess if so, that's a great opportunity for these types of coaches. But they're not the people I'll choose to work with.

15 Every Shot is Fresh

One of the things that I've learned in my Archery journey is to treat every single shot as if it's my first.

No matter whether I scored badly on the last shot, or my release wasn't as good as it could be, or I got distracted about what I'll be having for dinner, or I'm starting to tire after 90 minutes of shooting.

Whatever happens in each shot, the next one is fresh. It's a new opportunity to do it better. To do it 'correctly'. To breathe, to keep good form, to act positively and smoothly.

Allowing errors to propagate to later shots is the quickest way to perform badly.

So will we take the same attitude into our business?

Rejected on a sales call? The next one is fresh.

Had a bad morning? The afternoon is fresh.

We are constantly given the chance to have a fresh start; to ditch the baggage and be our best self.

Will we take the opportunity?

16 Create An Asset

Whenever you answer a question or give advice, you can create an asset.

If it's the first time the question has come up, systemise the answer.

A great example is someone who Bcc'd me on a bulk email today. I was able to reply by asking him to "listen to my Effective Email Marketing podcast with Lee Callender, starting at 09:40 (and particularly the bit at 11:35)"

No need to get emotional. No need to rant.

Just use the asset I've already created.

Can you do the same in your business?

—

[Bonus note: The book you're holding in your hands right now exists solely *because of the re-use of assets. What assets do you have in your business and life that can be re-used to reach a wider audience, or to reach them in a different way?]*

17 Sometimes The Room Isn't For You

I went to a one-day seminar on Wednesday. It was about property.

By the first break I realised that the room wasn't for me, but I'd already picked up some amazing nuggets on how to grow myself and my business.

So what should I do?

Sit in the room for the rest of the day and lose the will to live?

Or get out now and take action on the things I've learnt?

Naturally I did the latter, and suggest you do to.

There's nothing wrong with being deliberate about your actions. And nothing wrong with recognising when to cut your losses and get on with something more valuable.

18 The Pivot Points

Can we look back and recognise the important *pivot points* in our lives?

When did it all change? When did our mindset shift, and we realised there was more available?

When did our journey to "level up" begin?

Can we go back and re-create those feelings we felt when we had the "aha!" moment? Can we find new pivot points?

19 Select Yourself

95% of people either struggle, get by or just about grow themselves and their business.

This means that only 5% are really successful. They focus on the direction they want to take and push themselves in that direction.

So the chances of being successful are small, right?

No.

You see... the 95% are drifting. They are waiting for their circumstances to be right, or waiting for someone to come along and help them, or waiting for the "magic pill" that will make their life change without having to do the difficult stuff.

The 5% are self-selected.

They have *chosen* to be in the 5%. They "do the stuff" even when they don't feel like it. They act in spite of fear. They have a "see what happens" attitude.

It is easy to be in the successful 5% – just commit, today.

Yes, you'll go through pain, heartache and times when you have no idea what you're doing. You'll find that you stop hanging round with certain people, and start spending more time with others. You'll find that certain parts of your life will be left behind, and that may cause grief. These are all things we have to deal with when we decide to be in the top 5%.

But the key point here is that no matter what happens, your commitment means that you're *already* a success.

Select *yourself.* Because no-one else is going to.

20 Best Selling

Robert Kiyosaki talks about 'best selling' in his book Rich Dad, Poor Dad[3].

There's a big difference between "best-writing" and "best-selling".

Sure the writing (or whatever we do) has to be good. But if we don't tell anyone about it, nobody benefits.

Will we feel the constant need to improve what we do, or can we just change how we talk about it?

---

3. Rich Dad Poor Dad, Robert Kiyosaki, ISBN: 978-1612680194

21 The Path Includes Pain

When we learn to ride a bike, we graze our knee. We put disinfectant on it and it stings.

But when we grow up and want to learn more about life—how to run a business, how to get better clients, how to act fearlessly, how to get what we want—we're averse to grazing our knee. We don't want the sting.

What we don't realise is that all growth includes pain of some sort. And all remedies to our pain involve a stinging sensation.

So we have a choice...

22 You Don't *Find* Time

A recent conversation...

"I'd love to do X, but I just can't find the time."

"You don't *find* time, you create it."

"But I don't have any to create."

"How many hours per week do you spend watching American drama series?"

"About four or five."

"*There's* your time."

23 Everybody Is Doing The Right Thing

I truly believe that everybody is doing the right thing. Why would they do anything else?

So why do so many people do wrong, or evil? Or drift? Or get addicted?

Because "the right thing" is being filtered through:

Their Blueprint – what they've learnt in their upbringing

Their Environment – the external pressures placed on us

Their Ego – who they believe themselves to be

If we transcend our Blueprint, Environment and Ego, we can make better decisions that benefit all humankind instead of serving our prejudices and fears.

Will we commit to doing what's right? Not just what's right for us, right now?

24 Oars

In his book, Wink[4], (which I highly recommend) Roger Hamilton talks about oars. And it struck me recently just how important this concept is.

His premise is that when you're rowing, what you do when the oars are out of the water is as important, if not more, than what you do when they're in.

We all work hard. Do we *rest* hard as well? Do we truly recuperate and recharge? Do we get the angle of our oars right so when they go back in the water they pull effectively and efficiently?

Do we plan when it's quiet, so that next time it's busy we're on it?

---

4. Wink, Roger James Hamilton, ISBN: 978-9810583828

25 Missing The Obvious

I met my second wife over a year before I met my first. Ok, she was spoken for, so wouldn't have registered on my radar.

But it still took almost a year after splitting with my first to notice that my second was completely and absolutely the woman for me. I'd known her as a friend for 8 years by now.

Crazy.

Sometimes the obvious is right under our nose and we completely fail to see it.

(It is not coincidental that we became single at the same time... but that is a story for tomorrow's journal...)

26 Framing

There's a saying: "Things turn out best for those who make the best out of how things turn out."

And I have to say, framing is *everything*.

How we choose to look at events in our lives is completely responsible for our level of happiness.

For example, I had some "interesting times" in 2007. My wife and I were good friends with another couple. It seems my wife was 'better' friends, you might say, because she ended up leaving me for the guy in the couple.

Now that could have been disastrous, right? And I have to say it wasn't an easy time in my life.

However, it turned out that—as yesterday's journal alluded—I actually got on famously with the remaining friend (heck... we had a lot in common by now!) and after around eight months of being a blind idiot (me, that is), I asked her out.

We've now been married for nearly seven years. And, actually, everybody involved ended up with the best solution.

Not a disaster at all. By a long shot.

Can we see each of the events in our life as a gift of some sort? Even the ones that don't seem so marvellous at the time?

We don't *have* to… but if we don't, we could spend a lot of it miserable.

❧

27 Rewards

When we set up rewards for getting our tasks done, we send ourselves a subtle message...

"Your task is a chore."

The task is boring or unpleasant and the reward is there to help us get through the unpleasantness; to make it more palatable in some way.

Is that because we don't want to do the task? Why would we do something we don't want to do?

Surely each and every action should:

a) Bring joy in itself.

or

b) Be part of a greater purpose that makes it meaningful.

Should our reward not be in the future, but to be in *the action itself*? Is our reward not just simply the joy knowing that we're doing the right things, things that matter and giving our all in doing those things.

Let's *live* our rewards.

28 Ask For The Business

I know... sometimes it seems crass or desperate to ask for business.

But if we can genuinely help someone with a problem they have, why would we keep it to ourselves?

There are annoying, car-salesy, cold-cally ways to ask for business. And there are smart, pressure-free "need any help with that?" ways.

Let's commit to asking. But as a *favour* to our prospects, not as an annoyance.

29   What We Teach Our Kids...

School. Teaches our kids how to be obedient and good little factory workers.

(Nobody noticed that it's now the 21st century and factories aren't really around much).

And then gives them the summer holiday off to gather the crops.

(The agrarian age ended over 200 years ago).

So what—in the 21st Century, the time of greatest opportunity in history—could we be teaching our kids?

• **Money** – What it is, and what it isn't (for starters, it certainly isn't real).

• **Being Human** – AI will replace humans in ninety percent of what we do. Our only unique factor will be *the fact we're human.*

• **Detecting Truth** – We're in a post-truth world. Knowing *who* and *what* is genuine will be massively helpful.

• **Self Direction and Responsibility** – Recognising that we are responsible for our own attitudes and destiny.

• **Attention** – Where to spend our energy and attention for the most benefit (it probably isn't facebook or snapchat).

Anything else?

30 Get Stupid

Recently I was working on a minor re-brand and a new business card after a little course correction in my business.

I find that sometimes the way to get out of the box, to break out of your own self-imposed 'norm' is to just *get stupid.* So, I intentionally worked on the most ridiculous business card I could possibly create.

I wasn't planning to *use* this card. But what did the process do for me?

It helped me to break out of all the preconceptions of what I thought a card should look like, and allowed me to create from scratch without filtering out potentially good ideas because "we've never done it that way before".

Try it. Get stupid sometimes.

31 They Will Laugh

Yes, they might.

Is that any reason not to bring your gifts to the world?

They won't *all* laugh, and those gifts might be exactly what's needed for those who don't...

32 Two Mindsets

Recently I was at a Young Enterprise competition with the team I'm mentoring and I had chance to talk with one of their tutors.

Here's the tutor's mindset:

I always say "*when* you get through" to my teams. I don't want them to think they might not be selected.

Here's the underlying message:

You are entitled to get through no matter how good or shoddy your work is.

I found I really couldn't get on board with this, and stuck with my own message:

"*If* the judges decide to put you through".

The underlying message:

You are at the whim of the judges on the day and there is nothing you can do to control that. However, if you have done your very best, then whether you get through or not you can hold your head up and be proud of what you've achieved. If you've cut corners and done less than your best, you'll be upset if you don't get through and lucky if you do.

Who do you think has the healthiest message? Is my message too advanced for 18-20 year-olds? What message do you tell yourself?

❦

33 Why The Gurus Are Wrong

Ok, they're not really wrong. But they're not always totally *helpful*.

You see, the 'gurus' tell you do this, or do that.

Sure, it worked for them. It might not work for you.

So by all means test what they're suggesting, but the only thing you can really trust is yourself and your data, and your own values.

34 The Two Types of People

I had two conversations recently, on the same day.

One was along the lines of: "I'd really like to do that, but I just can't find the time."

The other was: "Wow. I'd better delete facebook from my phone and get on with it."

Guess who's getting where they want to be...?

35 The Joy of Creative Goal Setting

I knew a wonderful woman about 10 years ago, and I realised that even though I'd known her a long time she was actually the 'girl for me'.

But how should I approach? This stuff is terrifying, right?

I was, at the time, making use of a website called "43 Things" where you could publicly share goals and work on them.

So I set a goal... "Get Rejected"

Now here's a situation I couldn't lose.

I would either: a) succeed in my goal, or b) fail – but "get the girl".

I'm happy to say I failed.

What creative goal could you set yourself to help you get the difficult stuff done?

(*I didn't know about the law of attraction then, and might be tempted to keep away from a negative goal like that in future. But hey, it worked so I'm not complaining!)

❧

36 Have You Checked All The Pockets?

I experienced an Escape Room for the first time at the weekend. Really good fun... plenty of searching, puzzling and a little unsanctioned short-cut through lock-picking (always handy to have diverse skills, don't you think?)

But we became royally stuck at one point. We knew we needed a key. We knew we'd checked everywhere.

One of our party was wearing a utility vest we'd found in the room.

"Have you checked all the pockets?", we asked.

"Yes", she replied.

I took the vest and checked all the pockets again. Ok... no key.

A third member of the party took the vest. "Here's the key. In the pocket."

Sometimes it pays to have more than one set of extra eyes on a problem!

37 Getting In Early

Something came up in my Platinum Master Mind this month... one of the members has found an excellent way to get in to her clients before they ever need her service.

She has a strong niche of ideal clients. And she provides free (or very affordable) guides on just how to get started in that particular business.

Smart.

So they not only get to set up their business and be successful but there's only one company on their mind when they're in the market for the service she provides.

Trust is built over time. How can you start building trust with your potential clients before they even need your service?

38 "Average" is a Myth

Here's a trap that's easy to fall into; and it's a fundamental error that's in denial of how the world works.

Let's say you want to earn £200,000 from 20 clients next year.

That's pretty simple, yes? £200,000 divided by 20 is an average of £10,000 per client.

And that's the error.

Check the results for past clients. I bet you never get a flat average. You'll most likely get an 80/20 curve.

So the real numbers* for £200,000 from 20 clients is:

One client at £3,539

One at £3,699

Then £3,875, £4,070, £4,289

And so on up to the top three...

One at £18,140

One at £25,720

...and the "king of the castle – when they say jump, ask how high?" client at £46,720.

When we fight the 80/20 principle and try to work with human-created rules like "averages" we will struggle.

When we honour the principle, it will look after us well.

(*Give or take... this is not an exact science!)

39 Seven Years

It's my seventh wedding anniversary today, and it just reminded me of a really important rule to live by (that I finally picked up on the second time round!)...

Don't settle for second best. Go for what you want because you are worth it.

And act fearlessly. Risk looking like an idiot.

40 I Wish I Would...

Ever find yourself saying "I wish I would..."

...stop doing that.
...get more done.
...be better at networking.

Here's a question... just who is the "I" that is doing the wishing?

If the answer interests you, have a read of The Power of Now[5] by Eckhart Tolle. A fascinating insight into who "I" am and, indeed, who "I" am not.

---

5. The Power of Now, Eckhart Tolle, ISBN: 978-0340733509

41 You Are NOT Your Customer

Something that's often forgotten by small businesses, and particularly by the *staff* of small businesses…

"I'd never spend £400 on a pair of glasses", say the optical sales staff. And so they put up resistance on behalf of the client.

They never once think that the client might love the opportunity of spending £400 on a pair of glasses.

We all spend smart money and we all spend stupid money, and most importantly we all get the choice of what to spend it on.

Let's allow our customers to make that choice…

42   Pushy Sales

Who hates pushy salespeople?

You have your hand up? Yep. Thought so.

We sometimes resist the necessary job of selling because we've experienced so much bad salesmanship in the past.

We don't want to be like that person. We don't want to be the pushy idiot.

But we're missing the point slightly.

You see, when sales are done well, we don't even notice them. We call it "being helped" or "getting what we want or need".

We only notice the badly done stuff.

So let's begin our journey into *helpful* sales; into helping people get what they want and need.

A great place to start is Maxwell Maltz's book *Zero Resistance Selling*[6].

---

6. Zero Resistance Selling, Maxwell Maltz, ISBN: 978-0735200395

43 Respecting Ourselves

I'm not talking about the rapper's "Respec'" here.

I'm talking about respect. Respecting our choices. Respecting our boundaries. Respecting our genius. Respecting our values. Respecting our time.

Until we respect ourselves and our choices and our boundaries and our own genius and our values and our time, we can't expect anyone else to respect them.

Let's become clear with ourselves.

What will we no longer stand for? What will we no longer let ourselves get away with?

Let's *live* our respect for *ourselves,* and we will earn the respect of others.

44 Your Dashboard

So, you're driving along the motorway and suddenly you find the engine cuts out and you can't steer. How could this happen?

By not checking your dashboard.

It's the same in business. We all need a dashboard of the most important figures, and to keep our eye on it. Depending on our business, we may need to look every five minutes, every day, weekly or maybe monthly.

But we must look. Because otherwise we find ourselves with the equivalent of no fuel. Or an overheated engine. Or a blown-up gearbox.

When I last failed to look at my dashboard—embarrassingly recently, I might add—things went a little wayward. And when I caught up, it was abundantly clear why they'd gone that way.

If you don't have a business dashboard, I implore you to stop what you're doing right now and create one. It doesn't have to be fancy. It will evolve.

But *do* get started.

45 The Fear of Pricing

One of the most common things I come across in business owners is the fear around pricing strategy, and I've been there.

Firstly, we basically have no idea how to set our prices do we? There's no "magic answer".

So we have to make it up.

The quickest way to lose this game is to have a look at what everyone else is charging and charge about the same (or worse, charge less).

But if we're going to make our prices higher, the fear kicks in.

Won't our clients object? Won't we end up with no business, and lose our homes and starve to death?

(Not saying that fear is rational here... our fear has this habit of seeing the worst possible scenario).

The key is to provide *value*. And understand how much value we're providing, and how much—in cash terms—people will pay for that value.

And recognise that the environment we sell in will have as much impact on our revenue as the product or service we're selling.

✻

46 Headlines

The press have a lot to answer for.

Imagine if, instead of "Three People Stabbed", the headline read "0.000000046% of the UK population stabbed"

This isn't to minimise the impact on those three people and their families at all. But it does put it in perspective.

If we're going to insist on reading the headlines—not reading the news at all is my favoured route—we should at least apply our 'perspective' filter in order to counteract the press's apparent need for disproportionate sensationalism.

Chasing Up

I ordered a new PC recently. And the service from the courier was—how shall we put it?—less than exemplary.

After a near 'house-arrest' of 36 hours, and very unhelpful tracking status messages I decided to chase them. A hopefully-not-too-grumpy email later (to the original supplier, the logistics company and the local partner) and guess what? Priority delivery, a one-hour time window and amazing tracking suddenly became available.

I guess that it is 80/20 behaviour to only put effort into those who chase.

But it's not so classy, right?

I remember vividly in my photography business, not-coincidentally around the time it started to really take off, making a commitment one day: "No customer ever chases us up. We are *always* ahead of them."

And that commitment has served me well ever since.

48 Restrictive or Liberating

My wardrobe is pretty minimal – though I haven't *quite* gone to the levels of Mark Zuckerberg or Tom Scott, yet.

The subject came up in one of my sessions with my coach, and my coach asked "Do you find it restrictive?"

To which I replied… "No, actually. I find it very liberating never really having to think about what I'm going to wear."

And then it struck me.

The 'default diary', or scripting one's day.

I've always resisted the idea of being told (even if by myself) what I'm going to be doing with every second of the following day.

But I also know that many, many successful people do just that.

And what struck me was the link between the wardrobe and the to-do list.

What if I were to see it as an act of *freedom* to have my day scripted. So I don't have to worry about "what's next"?

Do you script your day? Would it be restrictive or liberating to do so?

꽃

49 Should I Tell Them?

"I saw a business making a big mistake; one that will cost them time and money... should I tell them?"

Difficult question, isn't it?

When the issue doesn't affect me personally—if it isn't a cutomer service issue, for example—I tend to follow Rule #1 from The Rules of Life[7], "Keep It Under Your Hat".

Nobody likes to be preached at. They're probably not ready to hear what you have to say. And they'll probably resist anything you do say to them.

Just get on with your life, be the good example, and if they ask how you're doing it, then and only if you deem wise, tell them what you've done.

It's certainly one way to look at it.

(The irony of my telling you this has not been lost on me, by the way)

---

7. The Rules of Life, Richard Templar, ISBN: 978-1292085609

50 The Car-Boot Microcosm

I had a big old declutter recently, and figured there was enough stuff to go for a car-boot sale.

I knew that I wasn't going to get the best prices, but figured that most stuff could just go for a quid or two, and on a few high ticket items I'd hold out for a good price and sell privately if I ended up taking them home.

Had a ball trying all the fun sales tactics, banter and segmentation with a high footfall.

And I have to say, the 80/20 was strong…

£120 made in the first hour (before the sale even officially opened)

£20 in the next hour

and £10 plus change in the next two hours.

If we could have left earlier, we would, but we were dependent on those around us packing up first.

Was it worth it? Yes! But I would never do it for a living.

51 How To Become an Insufferable Cretin

One of the most interesting things about the car-boot sale I talked about yesterday…

We were testing the stall to see which items would draw the most people in so we could begin cross-selling, up-selling and so on.

One test was to put Felix Denis's excellent book *How To Get Rich*[8] right at the front of the stall.

Well… that was a lesson in mindset.

From the reactions it garnered, you'd think we'd placed *"The Ultimate Guide to Becoming An Insufferable Cretin"* in plain view.

This is one of the major dichotomies of the world…

"I'd love to have more money" vs. "People with money are insufferable cretins."

---

8. How To Get Rich, Felix Dennis, ISBN: 978-0091921668

While people believe the latter their subconscious will never allow them to have the former, however much they think they want it.

But it's fine because it'll be the rich people's fault.

(A good way to get past the mindset, incidentally, is to read a book that's on my 'regular reading rota': Secrets of the Millionaire Mind[9])

---

9. Secrets of the Millionaire Mind, T. Harv Eker, ISBN: 978-0749927899

52 The £21,000 Birthday Card

It was a simple request... But let's set the scene.

After a cocktail or two on the 52nd floor of the Shard (recommended... awesome view!) I hot-footed across town to the watch boutique of a relatively well-known(!) department store.

Tried on a few watches and found a corker. Really beautiful. Exquisite craftsmanship. Smart, but nicely understated.

The price tag: £21,000.

Ok... it won't be my *next* watch, but you know, when I feel like a treat... I'll keep it on my radar.

"Certainly, sir", says the sales associate. "Can we get some details from you and when you come back we'll know exactly which one you want?"

"No problem."

I fill in the form, leaving the "date of birth" field blank.

"Can we have your date of birth, please?"

"Sure… but only if you send me a birthday card. You know, the deal's off if I don't receive a card."

"No problem.", and with that the associate writes "Birthday Card" next to my date of birth.

No card arrived.

I guess the lesson is that if you're going to push 80/20 to its limits and offer a truly premium service, you'll want to make sure your systems work perfectly; even with bespoke requests.

Either that or they actually don't care about the £21k. Also possible.

53 It's All Relative

A couple of years ago I took a pair of back-to-back holidays, firstly in Norway then hotly followed with a week or so in Switzerland.

After I returned I went to the local pub with my darling wife, ordered two pints, didn't really listen to the price and absent-mindedly handed over two £10 notes.

"Um... it's only £7", said the server.

Oh, um...

You see, it really is all relative. In Switzerland, I was accustomed to paying something over £5 per drink. In Norway I'm confident that £20 would have struggled to buy a couple of pints.

Give it a month and I'd think £20+ would be a *ridiculous* price to pay for a couple of drinks; certainly at the local pub.

We are conditioned by the environment that we buy and sell in. And that conditioning lingers.

54 A New Habit

As designers build addiction into everything they design*, it's time for us to learn a new habit if we're to stay productive.

That habit is:

Press "off" instead of "next".

Do not underestimate the importance of this. Learn it before it's too late.

(*Don't believe me? Check out *Evil By Design*[10] and *Hooked: How To Build Habit-Forming Products*[11])

---

10. Evil By Design, Chris Nodder, ISBN: 978-1118422144

11. Hooked: How To Build Habit-Forming Products, Nir Eyal, ISBN: 978-0241184837

55 Put The Social Media Down...

Fifteen things you could do instead...

▸ Interact with the people around you.
▸ Phone a relative.
▸ Plot your escape from a life situation that you hate being in.
▸ Draw, paint or doodle.
▸ Start that thing you've been putting off.
▸ Absolutely nothing.
▸ Catch up with an old friend.
▸ Revitalise that old hobby you loved doing.
▸ Learn something.
▸ Contribute time to a cause.
▸ Look around you and realise how lucky you are.
▸ Look around you and fix the most annoying thing.
▸ Breathe. Really breathe.
▸ Write a page of your book.
▸ Do something that makes your life or business 1% better.

56 Loosen Your Grasp

One of the biggest things I learnt about setting and achieving goals is to hold them loosely.

Grab them too tightly and you strangle them.

Hold them gently and look after them well, and they will be yours.

Kids Have It Right

Look at kids. They're able to be rock stars, space travellers, trees, caterpillars... whatever they *want* to be.

Why do we forget how to embrace the world of infinite possibility once we grow up?

Just because many people have said "no" and many have said "shouldn't you be more realistic", and many of our attempts have failed, it's no excuse to give up dreaming.

What do you want to be? Just go for it!

58 The Unrelated Stuff

Sometimes there are tasks on our to-do list that are unrelated to our business and our success.

But while they sit there, they take mental space, and take our most important asset: our attention.

Sometimes it's worth doing those things. They don't even need to be 'Frogs' (you've heard of *Eat That Frog*[12], yes?)

Get them done, then give 100% of your attention to the stuff that matters.

---

12. Eat That Frog!, Brian Tracy, ISBN: 978-1444765427

59 Kate Bush

I saw a documentary about Kate Bush.

Now, whatever you think about *Wuthering Heights*, you have to admit she's a total genius.

And two characteristics really shone out of the documentary...

1. **She writes music for herself.** If other people like it, great. If not, well never mind. She never wrote anything to please others.

2. **She's "happy to remain silent until there is something to say".** She'll leave four, six, even twelve years between albums and we'll hardly hear a thing until the new work is ready. In a world of media noise, this is refreshing.

Worth considering.

Your Money or Your Life

When we're using online tools we must choose what we pay with.

If we pay with money, the supplier's interest is in providing us with something useful that helps us.

If we don't, their interest is in addicting us to their product so they can get advertising revenue. They purposefully take our attention and our self-worth, and our time with our family, and our sleep.

If we don't pay with money, we pay with our life.

61 Figuring out what you want...

One of the reasons we allow others to spoon-feed us what 'success' looks like is that it's just *easier*.

If we just chase the money, the car and the fancy house we don't have to risk *thinking*.

We don't have to risk discovering we might be greedy. We don't have to dig deep and figure out what really matters to us.

But if we want freedom—and freedom is something I stand for unapologetically—we're going to have to do the work.

62 Don't Trust Small Datasets

If you're challenged to get the best score against the world darts champion, but you can choose how many darts you throw, what's the best strategy?

Ask for one dart.

There's a chance he might mess up. And there's a chance *you'll* get lucky.

The more darts you throw, the closer you get to a true picture of your skill.

But we'll still beat ourselves up when we have three sales meetings and two turn us down.

If we want the true picture, we must keep going and get enough data to give the full story.

63 One Good Test

Wernher von Braun (yes, it *is* rocket science) said:

"One good test is worth a thousand expert opinions."

We so often get stalled on trying to figure out what we *should* do... Learning more and doing less.

The answer is simple. If it's a choice of A or B, then do both and see which is more effective.

64 What you *must* do before 8:00am if you want to succeed...

I'm going to reveal the biggest secret in business to you today, by telling you what you *must* do before 8:00am if you want to be successful...

The answer is: *whatever the heck you like.*

Sleep if you like. Get up and go out networking. Read the paper. Or meditate. Or get to the gym. Or any combination.

Find that pattern that works for you and don't feel you have to do the same as everyone else, or what all the gurus are telling you to do (because their advice conflicts anyway).

And this applies for every moment of your life and business. Try stuff. Make mistakes. Find what works, and do more of it.

65 Options

We often believe that freedom comes from more options. More stuff. More distractions.

But when we start stripping away those options—the ones that don't bring us joy, that take us away from the things that really matter—it leaves room for the important ones to *breathe*.

We loose our death-or-glory grasp on our life and let *ourselves* breathe.

And when we breathe, we really start to live.

Reducing our options to the few that genuinely matter brings us true freedom.

The Great Audit

Ever done an audit?

I'm talking about an audit of yourself, your life, your beliefs and your belongings?

We seem to collect baggage and clutter in all of those areas. And sometimes it's worth having an audit and purge of those items that are no longer serving us.

I'm on my belongings at the moment.

I thought I'd struggle to find anything because I'm the first to say I hate "stuff" and I don't have anything I don't need.

And yet, I'm still finding boxes and drawers and shelves of "stuff" that serves no purpose other than to be in the way, to take mental space, and to not fulfil its purpose.

In my first book, The 80/20 Blueprint, I talk about the "Spring Clean" method of discarding the least useful stuff first. And this applies in every aspect of business and life. It brings the start of that 'breathing space' that I spoke about yesterday.

67 Joy

...and when you've given your things, your mind and your business space to breathe you will find those small things that bring you true joy.

Real, deep down, *heartfelt* joy.

68 Someone Has The Money

If you'd like to earn more for the work you do, know this...

Someone out there has the money.

80/20 says that one in five customers will spend four times the money.

One in twenty five will spend sixteen times the money.

Someone out there is looking for you, and massively values what you provide to the world. Go find them and reap the rewards.

69 Unsubscribe, don't delete.

I see so many inboxes that are completely inundated with emails, and there's one simple habit that can undo that situation.

Too many people hit 'delete' or 'archive' on the emails they don't want when all they have to do is hit the 'unsubscribe' button instead.

Sure, it takes a few seconds longer. But no longer than deleting the next ten unwanted emails.

After that you're in credit, timewise, for your habit.

And then your inbox starts to clear. And then you can breathe once again.

Seriously. Do it for *you*.

70 Nightmare Customers

It's 2017 and there is no longer any excuse for putting up with nightmare customers.

Just what is a nightmare customer? Put simply it's some-one whose world-view, values and goals are so out of line with yours that there is frustration and conflict.

(Maybe they don't value paying good money for good service, maybe they don't trust you, maybe you don't trust them – whatever the case, neither of you are wrong, just mismatched)

We now have the ability to reach a global audience, so we can find, attract and hang round with the people who *do* get our values.

So it's our fault if we're attracting or hanging on to the wrong customers. No-one else is to blame.

71 Your Past Self

While speaking at The Entrepreneur's Institute on Wednesday, I was asked "If you could go back in time, what advice would you give to your seventeen-year-old-self?"

Here's my reply:

"I'd hide from my seventeen-year-old-self and say nothing. Because if I said anything it could change his path, and I wouldn't be where I am today. I am completely content with where I am right now.

It's much more valuable, I think, to get to know your future *self—the person you want to be in 20 years from now—and take advice from him.*

Your seventeen-year-old self can't do anything about the advice you give him. Your present self can certainly act on the advice from your future self."

I have spoken about this in my book "Discover Your 80/20 Vision", so it was nice to have a lucid answer which, incidentally, I still fully stand by.

72 Duh

I had a session with my coach on Friday.

The problem I wanted to solve was the clarity of my message to my market.

I was frustrated because I work with my clients on simplicity and clarity, yet I couldn't find a simple, clear message for myself.

"Erm...", said my coach, "could your message be 'simplicity and clarity'?"

That's why we have a coach, folks!

73 Artificial Intelligence

Artificial Intelligence isn't all that intelligent.

Sure, it's getting extremely powerful, and can solve problems quicker than any human being, and come up with better solutions.

But intelligence doesn't lie in the solving of problems. Intelligence lies in defining *the problem.*

Let's look at YouTube's algorithm.

YouTube's algorithm is designed to show you more of what you love—whether that's comedy, epic fails or cute sea otters—and less of what challenges your worldview. That way you spend more time clicking 'next' and their advertisers sell more stuff. And that way YouTube (or Google who owns it) makes more money.

Very clever.

But it's not that *intelligent.* It's not a problem that actually matters to *us.*

Let's all put our energy and intelligence into defining the problems we're solving and checking if they matter.

74 What Do We Need?

What do we truly need?

Air and food.

What about shelter? Nice, but we don't *need* it. Companionship? The same.

Clothes? Handy for societal decency. Not actually a requirement.

Security and safety? Again, nice, but not needed.

When we pare back to what we really need, those big cars, fancy houses and stacks of cash in the bank take on a new meaning.

I'm not saying we shouldn't have those things. It's fine to have them. It's fine to want them. We can choose what we want and go get it.

But when we mistake *wanting* for *needing,* that's when the discontent begins.

75 Always The Right One

So, when I watched 'The Karate Kid' at the age of nine, there was a profound message that was lost on me. (Not surprising really, a nine-year-old only engages with the car polishing, fence painting, and karate action.)

But there's a scene where Mr. Miyagi is teaching Daniel how to trim a Bonsai tree.

"Close eyes", he says, "Picture perfect tree."

He then turns Daniel to the bonsai. "Now open eyes, and make like picture."

"But how do I know my picture is the right one?" asks Daniel.

"If it comes from inside you, *always* right one", replies Mr. Miyagi.

The same is true of all things. Once we discard what we think we *should* be doing, and what we think would please others, and what we've been *conditioned* to do, and our unconscious reactions caused by our emotions, we have the true message from inside ourselves. And that's *always* the right one.

76 Reaction

I'm going through an exercise in *presence* at the moment, and one of the most interesting things it's teaching is to "be with emotion."

So, when you feel that emotion rising, not to *react*. Not to lash out, or suppress it, or say 'yes' when you mean 'no', or fall into an unconscious reaction.

But to sit and breathe with the emotion for just a moment. Just one breath if necessary.

And then *respond* appropriately.

77 How to Stop Selling

Who hates sales?

Yep, me too.

Did you know that it's possible to stop selling altogether?

Selling suggests that you're trying to coerce someone into having something they don't want, for *your* gain.

How about just providing outstanding value?

Give. Serve.

And when people say "How can I get more of this?" you explain how. And gratefully receive the rewards.

78 Authenticity Revisited

I've written before about authenticity and how it helps us to preserve our energy.

But the next level is realising what 'authentic' really means.

Step one is "be who you *think* you are".

Then you realise that years of indoctrination, conditioning and trying to fit in have taken their toll.

You might not be who you think you are. You are probably much more awesome than that. Seriously.

And that's where the real work starts.

79 Mindset

We talk about having the right *mindset*. But sometimes it's not the *mind* that's needed.

In fact, the mind is entirely *incapable* of understanding and grasping some of the concepts necessary to lead an authentic life.

But "heartset" and "soulset" aren't catchy enough to get people engaged.

Drama

We're doing work that matters. If it didn't matter, we wouldn't be doing it.

So let's not get caught up in the drama. Let's not get distracted by hype. Let's not allow the fear of the masses and the media to derail us.

Let's spend all of that energy, instead, by continuing with our important work...

81 I Know

The other day I spent a very enjoyable five hours teaching archery to members of the public.

There were those who said "I know, I've done it before."

And there were those who said "I'm not sure, show me."

The latter, unsurprisingly, performed significantly better.

Let's remember to say "I know" less often, and "show me" more.

82 Only One

Whenever I have a prioritisation task, my go-to tool is *onlyone.io*

It's really simple (as you know, I like simple)

Type in your list. Press go. Pick which you would have/do/be if you could only have one.

And after a few head-to-head battles between your items, out pops a prioritised list for you to get started on.

I have no affiliation... it's just one of those tools that I use again and again... I love it, I hope you'll find it helpful too...

http://onlyone.io

83 Don't Worry About What Everyone Else Is Doing

I was at my Yoga class this morning and we were just in the midst of one of those moves... you know, *"if you're level 4, then balance on your left foot, rub your tummy with your right hand, stick your right foot on the top of your head and point the fingers of your left hand into the 9th dimension".*

As we wobbled and balanced and struggled to get into the 6th dimension, let alone the 9th there was a collective hesitation, a looking around, a feeling of "I wonder if I'm good enough"

And the instructor, sensing this said:

"Don't worry about what everyone else is doing. They're not worrying about *you*, I promise."

And she was right. And more to the point, she was right about all things.

Why do we get so hung up on whether we're doing it "right"; whether we're doing it the same as everyone else;

whether we're better, or worse, or smarter, or not good enough?

We're doing the stuff, in our way. And let's keep on doing it proudly and fearlessly.

84 Just a Mountain

"Before a man studies Zen, to him mountains are mountains and waters are waters;

After he gets an insight into the truth of Zen through the instruction of a good master, mountains to him are not mountains and waters are not waters;

But after this, when he really attains to the abode of rest, mountains are once more mountains and waters are waters."

When we first go into business we feel that we can just show up and people will gravitate to us.

Then we learn about marketing and influence and copywriting and tricks and tips. And we realise that if we just show up, people won't gravitate to us. We have to grab their attention, find the pain points, poke them until they bleed, then offer the 'magic' solution.

Then as we mature, we realise that actually, yes... we *can* just show up.

(Albeit a whole new level of 'showing up')

Create a Vacuum

A while ago I was in a gallery, and started chatting with the assistant.

"Yeah… we're kind of looking for something to go above the fireplace. We're not super-happy with the picture that's there at the moment. It's ok, but it's not brilliant…"

Her advice was swiftly given…

"When you get home, take the picture down straight away. Create a vacuum, and it will be filled."

And she was right. With the big blank space staring at us it was a matter of days before the perfect inspiration struck.

The same is true in everything. We put up with 'adequate' because it's *there*. It's easy. It doesn't need thinking about.

But when we discard the 'adequate', it makes room for the great.

86 The Radio Dial

I was asked "How can we be happy with so much pessimism around?"

And as I was answering I realised something...

The world is exactly like a radio.

There are any number of radio signals out there, flying through the air at all times. Right now there's a Russian show about politics, a French music channel, the shipping forecast and an aeroplane talking with the tower at Heathrow.

Grab a world-band receiver and turn the tuning dial and you can pick up any one of these channels.

Likewise, the world is handing us an almost infinite number of messages at all times; joy, depression, abundance, lack, rich, poor, positive, negative.

It is up to us to move our dial to tune into the messages that are most helpful.

87 Without The Froth

I overheard an interesting exchange at the counter of a cafe during a recent lunch…

"Hi. Can I have a frothy coffee, please? With no froth."

"A frothy coffee with no froth?"

"Yes, it gets caught in my moustache."

"Um… yes, I'll see what I can do."

Lesson 1: It's always worth asking. You might just get what you want.

Lesson 2: If you don't know what you're doing, accept the challenge, but acknowledge that it's a test.

88 Saying "Yes" When We Mean "No"

One of the biggest obstacles to success is saying "yes" when we mean "no".

Not only do we fill our time with things we don't want to do, but we also start to mistrust ourselves and question our decisions and commitments.

So let's say "no" when we mean it. And remember that "no" is a complete sentence.

89 The Opposite of "Good"

We spend a lot of our lives trying to be "good"; trying to please our forebears, parents, teachers, peers (or the echos of them from our youth)...

But being "good" limits us to the walls and boundaries that those people put in place. Probably for no other reason that they, themselves, were trying to be "good".

The opposite of "good" isn't "bad", because "bad" requires buying into the same walls and boundaries.

The opposite of "good" is "yourself".

You don't have to be *bad* in order not to be *good*. But to be *yourself*, you may need to break away from *good*.

90 Happiness In The Future

When we place our happiness in the future—if I can just get X, or after I've made Y-amount of money—then we will never find it.

There will always be a new goal and a new horizon.

We must be happy today. If we can't manage that, there's very little hope that we'll be able to find it further down the line...

The Secret to a Happy Life

Ok ok, there are no secrets.

Here's my formula to happiness that I'm living, breathing and working on daily (note: *working on* is a big part of the formula!)

Clarity, Simplicity, Freedom

1) Clarity – Know what you want and what's important to you, and why.

2) Simplicity – Pursue and appreciate what you have, and what's important.

3) Freedom – Don't allow past conditioning or peer pressure to stop you doing and appreciating what's important.

It's a simple formula. Not necessarily easy to implement. But certainly simple.

92 The World's Biggest Collection

Steven Wright has a joke:

"I have the world's largest collection of seashells. I keep it on all the beaches of the world... perhaps you've seen it."

It's funny. It's silly. And it hides a profound wisdom.

Appreciation without ownership.

Why do we need to accumulate and acquire all that 'stuff'? Why do we need to own stuff?

Since having a go on a potters wheel a few weeks ago I've become increasingly interested in ceramics. Do I feel the need to own any? No.

I have the world's biggest collection of ceramics. I keep it in the workshops, galleries and shops of the world.

Appreciation without the clutter. And the bonus is that other people can appreciate my collection too.

93 Abundance

What if we take yesterday's post about The World's Biggest Collection and apply it to money?

What if we accept that we, right now, have all the money in the world.

We just keep it in various places – other people's bank accounts, flowing through cash registers, lost down the back of furniture...

We might not be able to *control* all of it, but we can certainly *appreciate* it.

That, my friends, is abundance.

94 Listen

When do we truly listen? Not to other people, but to ourselves?

When do we listen to our body? When do we listen to our insight? When do we listen to the messages the world is telling us at every moment of every day?

We try to find happiness in the 'stuff', in the distraction, in the future...

But it's here now for the taking if we will just listen.

The Rhinoceros

The Rhinoceros is bashing at the door, and our fears have us holding it back with all of our might. We feel it... BANG... BANG...

BANG...

The door judders with each blow. Can we hold it any longer? It takes so much energy to hold the door back.

But what if it gets in?

What if the Rhinoceros is our true genius, and by letting it in we finally fulfil our purpose in life?

What kind of person will we be called to be?

Will we find out it's not as bad as we thought?

Dare we take the risk and open the door...?

96 Are We Sheep?

I was asked "Are we sheep?". Here's the answer I gave...

We are conditioned to follow the herd, yes.

We find comfort in doing what everyone else is doing, yes.

We chew grass like there's no tomorrow, even while standing in a field with more grass than we could ever eat. (Ever watched a sheep eating?)

Something like 95 to 98% of people are sheep. You can watch them unconsciously walking around, face in their phone, heart and soul suppressed, face wrinkled with worry, with their happiness firmly placed in the future – "when I just have this next shiny thing, I'll be happy"...

But we don't *have* to be sheep. There are those who choose to live apart from that world.

Some do it from the ego, "Look at me, I'm different, aren't I clever?"

Some do if from their heart, "My heart says this is right, even though I won't gain approval. My heart says that is wrong, even though everyone is doing it."

I'm currently learning the path of the heart. It invites ridicule and disagreement and bemusement. But when we know our truth—or are seeking it with all our heart—we no longer need to follow the herd.

Others who are following *their* truth will support us even if their truth is different, because they recognise the value of seeking and having our own truth.

97 Hustle

"Hustle" is the new stick for us to beat ourselves with.

If I'm not taking massive action there must be something wrong with me. If I'm not filling my life with *stuff*, if I'm not outperforming all those other people around me, if I'm not working every hour of the day and more…

Let me tell you straight… hustle is a symptom of the ego.

Who are we trying to please? Those around us? The ghosts of our parents (whether alive or no longer with us)? Our inner critic?

When we're quiet for long enough to find our core inspiration, there's no stopping us. We will work tirelessly for what matters.

But until then, let's not wear ourselves out on fools' errands.

"Hustle" is the new "Mine's bigger than yours".

The "Bear" Test

We humans have made our lives extremely complicated, so I have a little test I apply – the "bear" test.

And it goes like this:

Would a bear care about this problem?

If not, I recognise that this is a human-generated problem and not a 'real' problem (of survival, thriving and freedom)

An example: National borders.

A bear can walk across a national border with no problems. The bear doesn't care and the humans don't care. A human gets questioned at least, and shot at worst.

National borders do not pass the "bear" test. And problems that do not pass the "bear" test can be treated differently to the others.

99 The Novelty Paradox

If we are to be truly happy, we mustn't pin our happiness on the next shiny thing. Novelty wears off, as does the 'happiness' it brings.

But we must also avoid getting stuck in our ways. We should try new things regularly. Try new ways to do things.

That's the paradox.

Be, have and do the new stuff. But don't pin your happiness on it.

100 My Favourite Truth

My favourite "truth" is the following:

Nobody knows what they're doing.

The interesting thing is that almost no-one is willing to admit they have no idea what's going on. We end up thinking that we, alone, have no idea; that everyone else is somehow more equipped to deal with life, is 'better' than us, has the magic secret that we're missing out on.

But let's be real. Nobody really knows.

Start from there and we can make solid progress.

101 The "Time Debt" Crisis

Remember the financial crisis of 2008? Remember what caused it?

Too many people spending money they didn't yet have. (To buy things they didn't need, to impress people they don't like, if you believe the amusing quip)

And we've almost got that under control now. More people are aware of financial planning and budgeting. They understand how compound interest can work for them or against them; and whichever way it's working, it's very powerful.

But there's another crisis in our midst... the "time debt" crisis.

How far ahead is your diary booked? When's your next free weekend?

We have a tendency to book our diary further and further in advance. It's mid-July now, apparently the most common time for businesses to book their Christmas parties. Yes, really.

We search through our diaries for a free weekend... Ok, not this month... not next month... ok, three months' time... and then without realising we're exacerbating the situation, we commit to an appointment and write it in.

"Time Debt" is essentially committing to do something in the distant future, thereby removing choice and freedom when that time comes.

Are we going to take charge? Are we going to budget our time? Because time is far more valuable than money.

102 Grown-Up Conversations

Why do we shy away from grown-up conversations?

Is it because we might find out we're wrong? Or risk looking stupid? Or have a fear that the other person somehow knows better?

Or do we fear being 'told off' or 'called out'?

Or do we just not want to put the effort in to figure out what we want, what's important and where our boundaries are?

Is it easier to put up with sub-standard relationships and situations than to know ourselves?

Let's take the challenge this week to have one 'grown-up conversation' that we've been putting off. We'll discover that it wasn't as bad as we thought, and our self-worth will be hugely boosted by honouring what matters to us.

103 Escapism

Escapism is fine and dandy. You know, going to the spa or having the fancy stuff in your bath to make you feel better.

But have you noticed how that feeling doesn't last?

And that's the essence of Zen.

Rather than rely on external stuff to give us peace and harmony, we practice mindfulness whenever we can. And that allows us to bring peace and harmony into everything we do.

Then we don't need to escape.

104 Idiots...

We've all come across them. People who just don't "get it". Who bumble on and mess about and cock up our lives and drive us up the wall.

What if I told you they were actually messengers, trying to tell you something about yourself?

No?

Well, how about the fact there are hundreds and thousands of messages coming your way every moment.

Some, you resonate with, agree and see them as good. The majority you ignore – you are completely unaware that there's a potential message.

And some get on your nerves.

There's a reason for that.

If you're in a restaurant and the walls are painted red, you will either:

Like the red walls ("good" resonance)

Dislike/hate the red walls ("messenger" resonance)

Or you'll just not notice them at all.

So if you notice them, for whatever reason, it's because of something going on in *you*. And when you can tap into the message and figure out what it's trying to tell you, life becomes much easier.

Next time you meet an "idiot", try to figure out why you can't just ignore them. What does it say about you and your values? What's their message to you? Pay attention…

105 The Invisible Cage

It's said that Eastern cultures (Japan, China, Korea) are group-oriented, while Western cultures (UK, Europe, USA) are individual-oriented.

There's some truth in this, but I think it misses a very important point.

You see, we Western cultures *are* group-oriented, we're just more stealthy about it.

Go to Japan and you'll see workers doing group callisthenics in their workplace each morning. It's an *explicit* group orientation.

Whereas in the West, it's *implicit*.

We still expect people to 'fit in'. We still expect people to remain within our own comfort zones.

But rather than say anything, we just tut, shake our head, or passive-aggressively make their life difficult to keep them on track.

If we are to be free, we need to first recognise this invisible cage. And then we find that it isn't actually locked and we can swing the door open.

Stepping out of it is another matter... it takes time and courage.

106 Doing The Right Thing?

"How do I know if I'm doing the right thing?"

Here's the truth... are you ready...

Because you are doing it, it is *the right thing.*

Now that sounds just a little bit funny, doesn't it? How can it be the right thing just because you're doing it? Surely you must be able to do the wrong thing?

Well, here's the deal...

You've done a lot of 'things' up to now, right. Some have been 'right' and some have been 'wrong'. But if any one of them had been different, you'd be in a different situation today. You wouldn't be in the place you're at right here, right now.

And the place you're at right now is where you are meant to be.

All the mis-steps and less-than-classy moments along the way have built your character to the amazing, gifted, and wiser person that you are today. So, on balance, they were the right things to do, yes? Even if it didn't feel like it at the time.

Well, I'm offering you today, for one time only (!), the chance to accept that everything you do from this moment is also the 'right thing', whatever it looks like at the time.

107 Off-Peak Travel

As I sit in my 'batcave' listening to the traffic commuting outside, it strikes me that I have yet another of the things I wanted all along.

When we design our lifestyle, we make conscious choices to improve our situation. And this is a decision I made some time ago...

Only travel off-peak, where possible.

There's a reason I generally only meet my 1-2-1 clients after ten in the morning. It's not because I'm lazy, it's because I get two major benefits:

▸ I get to spend 90 minutes working on me and my business before anything else has the chance to potentially mess my day up.

▸ I get to remain stationary while the world is moving about, and then travel on empty roads when those busy people are all safely sitting behind their desks.

Is it reasonable to only meet clients after 10am? That's irrelevant. It's what I've chosen, for very good reasons. I show up more calm, more balanced and more able to do my job.

What conscious decision could you make today to have a positive impact on your life situation?

❦

108 Amazing

You are more amazing than you know.

Seriously.

In fact, I'll go one step further... you are more amazing than you can even fathom.

Every single person on this 'spaceship Earth' is a unique genius. They have a unique outlook, a unique perspective, and that perspective has immense value.

But we hide behind our fears. We hide ourselves because others might judge us. Or we might look stupid.

It's time to let that go...

Be a genius. Let your beautiful weirdness shine out like a ten million gigawatt light. Let others bathe in your light. They'll be too worried about how they look to worry about you anyway.

109 Very Fishy

You know, we hide ourselves for fear of criticism.

Here's a genuine one-star review of a fish restaurant I spotted recently:

"The fish had a strong fish taste"

I'd be pretty annoyed if my fish didn't taste of fish. It's hilarious.

So will we restrict ourselves so we don't attract these kinds of reviews? Or will we get on with it and accept them as part of life...

110 Progress

I was sitting outside in the garden at 3 o'clock the other morning, enjoying the universe with a cup of tea.

A couple of aeroplanes flew over—not low enough to be landing at my local airport, but not high enough to be going long-distance—and I first of all got to wondering where they were headed.

Then something struck me – just how far we've come.

There's a metal tube up there with two hundred people on it, flying at five hundred miles per hour through the sky.

Just take a moment to let that sink in.

Then bring it back to the more simple progress we have (if we are lucky enough to live in the developed world)... clean water delivered straight to our homes; shelter; political stability; plentiful food; cheap, warm and readily available clothing,

The list goes on and on.

We now live a life that our ancestors, even 100 years ago, would give their right arm for.

And yet we still find time to be discontent.

How is that possible?

Let's remember, with total gratitude, all the amazing stuff we have.

111 Marketing

There are two types of marketing, I guess. And if you've been following this journal for any amount of time you'll know that I've fallen out with one of them greatly.

The first sort is the simple "Let people know it's there" marketing.

If you're in a supermarket, think about carrots. They put the carrots out on a shelf and they put a sign near them saying (surprise, surprise) "Carrots"

The second sort is persuasion marketing. You know, getting into your prospective customers' psychology, interrupting their thought patterns, creating fear, uncertainty and doubt in their mind and then providing the 'magic' solution. This accounts for the majority of marketing out there (or the majority of the stuff you'd notice).

But consider this... what's so wrong with what they're selling that they have to try that hard to sell it?

Again, look in the supermarket. The stuff with heavy marketing is invariably bad for you. The cakes have persuasion marketing... "Go on! Be naughty!"... "Treat yourself, you deserve it..." This is a deliberate attempt to distract you from your deep-down instinct that the cakes are not going to serve you long-term.

The first step is to become aware of the messages being sent to you... if they're trying too hard, there's a good chance you don't need what's being sold.

And we can be aware of the messages we're putting out there too.

112 Dealing With Uncertainty

We live in an uncertain world, that's for sure.

I've spotted three basic patterns for dealing with this uncertainty...

1. We have a feeling that nothing is under control, and therefore give up trying. This leads to stagnation.

2. We strive to get *everything* under control. We create goals and rewards, we berate ourselves when we're not trying hard enough. This leads to anxiety, stress and palpitations.

But there is another way:

3. We *recognise* that nothing is under control – and that's *ok*. This requires a different kind of goal-setting... one of intention and attention. We set a loose intent as to how we'd like things to turn out, then we pay attention for opportunities to make it happen. And if we don't get our intent, we gratefully acknowledge that we received what we were 'meant' to receive, even if it wasn't what we thought we wanted.

113 Insanity

You've seen the 'train pushers' in Japan?

You know, those men and women with impeccable uniforms and white gloves, employed to shove people onto already-overloaded trains.

We look at that and we laugh. "How insane!", we say, "can't they see how crazy this is?"

And it is.

I wonder what *we're* doing that feels "normal", but is actually completely insane?

114 In Search of a New Perfection

I call myself a 'recovering perfectionist'. When I did a motivational drivers test many years ago, I was off the scale on "be perfect". I believe this comes from a combination of nature and nurture and it's held me back in a few ways (and been the source of much pulling of hair and gnashing of teeth) over the years.

So, how did my recovery begin?

It was by re-framing perfection by a little-known Japanese standard called 'wabi-sabi', a complicated concept that is impossible to translate... so I'll try now:

> *wabi-sabi celebrates the beauty in imperfection; it is the true perfection. It believes that 'perfect' perfection is, in itself imperfect due to a lack of soul, character, vulnerability, humanity. And so it gives us a new, attainable, perfection to strive for.*

The basics, for a simple Western understanding, are:

Nothing lasts
Nothing is finished
Nothing is perfect

And when we hold ourselves to these standard of perfection—instead of the unattainable, self-flagellating levels we're accustomed to striving for—we find that things immediately become easier.

We can park our car badly in the parking space and instead of spending an extra two minutes straightening it up, we can just mutter 'wabi-sabi', get out and continue with our day.

We can be weeding the garden and fancy a tea break, and go for that break with just a little corner of the garden un-weeded.

We can—to take a personal example—visit the highest points of 110 of the 132 counties in Britain and then decide "Actually, this isn't really fun any more. There are better hills that aren't county high-points. That'll do." and not force ourselves to drudge through the rest of them.

It's liberating, it's practical, and it is still a form of perfection – just a more healthy and helpful one.

115 De-Cluttering and Personal Growth

We collect a lot of clutter in our lives, and I'm not just talking material clutter. We collect paperwork, we collect grudges, we collect unfinished business and un-dealt-with situations.

The clutter we collect is physical, mental and emotional.

Some years ago, I decided to allow life to flow through me, and not get backed up, blocked and stuck. I hadn't really made the connection at the time between this concept and the clutter that had collected in my mind, body, memories and physical environment.

But when I began to de-clutter my physical environment it gave me that little bit of room to breathe. And in that breathing space it became apparent that I'd been collecting mental and emotional clutter.

They're a little harder—bad choice of word, but it'll do for now—to clear out.

Bit by bit, item by item, we examine our possessions, our beliefs, our grudges, our past hurts, our habits, our daily thoughts, and we decide if they're serving us or not. And if they're not serving us, we give them a quick 'hug' and send them on their way.

It's not a battle to have with ourselves. It's not a process that will ever be complete (as we know, nothing is finished). It's a continual, gentle discipline that gives us the mental, physical and emotional space to be our best selves.

116 A Path To Success

I know, I know. What's success? It isn't a destination...

But here's an interesting path we might consider...

1. Drop the unhelpful stories we tell ourselves about almost everything.

2. Take action.

Pretty simple, yes? We think that step 2 is the hard part, but if we do the work on step 1, step 2 is pretty straightforward.

117 Energy Providers

Most of us have some sort of energy sent to our home, yes? Gas, electricity...

And how do we pick a provider of that energy?

Quality of service? Cost? Reputation? Quality of energy?

(Does anyone actually check the *quality* of the energy coming in? If you do, let me know how!)

If we put physical energy aside for the minute and look at emotional and spiritual energy, there are a whole new set of providers that we might not have thought about...

Every single person, situation and thought we encounter is an energy provider. Those we encounter often are the key ones to think about for the moment.

Looking at each one, what is the quality of the energy they're providing?

And what is the cost of that energy?

Sometimes we need to switch providers. Not only our *physical* energy providers, but also those that provide our emotional and spiritual energy.

118 How Much Are You Worth?

Ever get that feeling...? What am I doing with my life? I'm not worthy? What's it all about...?

Well, let's do a bit of maths...

The average adult human weighs 62kg, and taking Einstein's e=mc², we discover that a 62kg human contains 5,572,282,108,168,269,368 joules of energy.

That's 1,547,856,141,157 kilowatt hours.

And at today's energy prices (12.5p/kWh) that means **our average human is worth £192,482,017,644** (if they can just convert that energy to cash as efficiently as a power station)

Even better, whenever they eat something they increase their worth hugely.

Ok... a bit silly, but interesting to consider...? And a great starting point when considering our 'true worth'...

(This is not an incitement to increase your value by embracing obesity: I don't think it quite works like that!)

119 Change Levels

When there's a problem to be solved, it is almost never a good idea to solve it at the same level that it occurs.

That's like replacing the damp wallpaper on our ceiling without plugging the leak in the roof.

Whichever way we go is valid... let's go up a level, or down a level, or even step sideways... let's not stick a plaster over the wound, but go and find its cause.

Then we won't keep running out of plasters. Or wallpaper.

120 How To Mediate

I believe that meditation is absolutely key to a content life, and that's why I meditate for fifteen minutes twice a day.

Except, out of all the people who actually meditate, I think I may be the *worst person in the world* at meditating (Or is that you? Entries on a postcard!)

So here are my top tips for poor quality meditation:

1. Make sure you meditate in a place with plenty of distractions so that you can procrastinate for 30-60 minutes before starting your session.

2. Make sure your timing mechanism is the most complicated possible – I find that a meditation app linked to a bluetooth speaker that always takes a few attempts to connect is best. It allows you to be sufficiently frustrated and non-centred when beginning your session.

3. Sit either cross-legged on the floor or a zafu so that your legs and back get distractingly uncomfortable during your session. Or alternatively sit in a swivel chair so

you can explore the joys of spinning around with your legs stuck straight out.

4. Make sure you're hungry before your session so you can get distracted by what you're planning to eat for your next meal, rather than sitting in peace.

5. Try to predict when your session will be ending. It's best if you remain locked firmly into 'clock time' while meditating so you don't get *too* lost in the present moment.

If you do all of these (as I do embarrasingly frequently), you'll be sure to get the *least* benefit from your meditation session.

But here's the important part... when you do any or all of these things and *don't give up,* slowly, over time, you still reap the benefits.

And through practice your ability to be still and calm improves; and eventually it begins to permeate your life.

Shortcomings—and the acceptance and forgiveness of them—are a huge part of the process.

121   Contradictions

Have you noticed how often we have to choose between contradictions?

I want X, but I also want Y... I want the cake, but I want to lose weight... I want to stand up for my rights, but I don't want to upset him/her...

It can drive us mad going round and round the contradictions, trying to resolve them.

And that's because we're looking in the wrong place.

The answer is very often in the middle. It's the paradox of the contradiction that allows us to create an answer.

There's a fascinating quick-read called *"Owning Your Own Shadow[13]"* that describes the paradox in detail.

---

13. Owning Your Own Shadow, Robert A. Johnson, ISBN: 978-0062507549

122 Self-Selection

There are those who complain about the 'successful' which is interesting because everything is available to these complainers to follow suit (or find their own 'success' path).

But even if you lay out the instructions in fine detail and list the tasks required and the order to do them in, you'll find that many will continue to complain and not take the actions required.

Whether through fear, self-doubt or other self-sabotaging methods, we have a huge tendency to stick where we are, with what we know and in our comfortable place of quiet misery.

We all have a choice... get busy complaining or get busy growing (to misquote The Shawshank Redemption).

What will we choose today? And who will we ask for help? Will we do the difficult work on the inner game?

123 Burn-Out

Why do we burn out? It's often because we care. We don't want to let anyone down, and we take on more responsibilities than we can reasonably handle. (If we don't do it, nobody else will, right?)

But there's another factor, and that becomes clear *after* we burn out.

That's the point where we show ourselves a "red card" and realise we have to start focusing on what's really important. Not the trifling things, not the drama, not helping those who are perfectly capable of helping themselves, or those who take no benefit no matter how much we help them.

We realise we need to put our own needs first, look after ourselves properly and start being intentional with our time and energy. We realise there are certain things we value above all others, maybe our family, maybe our health, maybe our hobby that keeps us centred.

The interesting thing is that within all of that lies the solution to not burning out in the first place.

The solution is to give ourselves permission to make those choices before the situation becomes critical.

Permission is all it takes sometimes. If not now, when?

124 Relationships

I've always said I'm really pleased I've never taken drugs to numb my emotions. I've just used a string of failed relationships instead! (and at various times overeating, dubious preferences, alcohol, you name it... but no drugs, so that's 'good')

As I move into presence there's something that has become truly obvious, and it relates to those relationships. And that obvious truth is:

Between two relationships, if we don't do the inner work, we'll just repeat the same story.

This does't just apply to romantic relationships; we must look at our relationships with friends, our business relationships – as a client or a provider, and our relationship with ourselves; it applies to *all* of our relationships.

It's not about *them*. It's about *us*, and how we perceive the world.

And if it's going wrong, it's a message to us to change our game.

And so if we don't change our own inner game, the world will keep showing up the same way until we get the message.

🌿

125 We Get To Choose

Sometimes, when we're in the thick of it, we forget that we get to choose *everything* about how we show up.

One of my Master Minders reported a few days ago that he'd been invited to take on a decent contract. His terms, made very clear at booking, are pre-payment only. The prospective client didn't pre-pay, they gave themselves 30 days credit (which we all know turns into 60 or 90 days in reality).

So what happened when the money didn't show up before the contract date?

No drama. No problems. A quick phone call to reiterate the terms, and the prospective client cancelled.

And my Master Minder? "Elated" is the word he used.

Sure, he's turning down some cash. But what would be the cost of earning that cash in hassle, stress, drama and admin?

We must never forget that we get to choose...

126 Goals

We coaches have to be very careful.

Imagine Mother Theresa had gone to a coach and said "I'd really like to be successful"

And the coach says "Great, what would you like to succeed at?"

And Mother Theresa says "Feeding the poor and looking after them"

And the coach says "That's not success. You need to systemise your work, and make plenty of money so you can buy a big house and a Ferrarri"

You get the idea.

We have to be very careful to help people reach *their* idea of success, not ours.

127 We Only See What We Want To See...

It's true... we only see what we want to see; even when we know differently.

Here's the proof...

We know that the moon is a big round rock in space, and we know that the stars are millions and billions of miles away.

But you try looking at the night sky and seeing anything other than a kind of dome with points of light stuck to it. Try seeing the moon as anything other than a circle (or crescent) stuck on the inside surface of the dome.

Even when we know what we're looking at, we're still sometimes incapable of seeing it.

And the same is true of all things.

128 Stop and Breathe

One of my Master Minders reported a huge success this week. She was about to embark on a marathon phone session to catch up with 160-odd people, when she decided to take ten minutes and breathe.

As she took time out, she considered "Is this the best way to do things?" And concluded perhaps not.

Inspiration struck and she put something in place that saved her making 50 of those calls.

That's a pretty good return on time invested.

We can all do the same. Next time we're about to take on a long task, let's just take 10 minutes beforehand to consider if we're going about it the best way. Worst case, we lose 10 minutes. Best case we recover minutes, hours or even days of time back.

129 War

The only way you can get people to go to war is to *make them forget that the people at the other end are humans.*

This is true of all strife, hate, conflict, drama.

Whatever conflicts we have in our lives—big or small— let's remember that those other people are humans just like us.

(It actually goes way deeper than this, but that's a rabbit hole we probably don't want to go down right now)

130 The Weekend

What is our weekend for?

Working? Catching up? Resting? Doing nothing? Filling with excitement?

Whatever we choose, let's do it deliberately and be present for every moment.

131 Just Borrowing It

I found some money the other day. Only a small amount, but it went into my wealth jar. I celebrated, as per *Secrets of the Millionaire Mind*[14]… "Yesssss!!!! Thank-you! I am a money magnet! You're mine!"

And then realised that it isn't really mine. I'm just borrowing it.

Borrowing it?

Well, yes. I'm just borrowing it until I either die, or exchange it for something else, or lose it, or have it stolen, or it melts in a house fire, or currency becomes obsolete…

It's not mine at all. And nor is anything else that I'm currently looking after.

Everything we have—material things, circumstances, relationships, luck, time—is just "borrowed for now". And when we realise that, we can allow ourselves to relax a little.

---

14. Secrets of the Millionaire Mind, T. Harv Eker, ISBN: 978-0749927899

132 The Fancy Stuff

There's a load of fancy stuff we can do to improve our life, our business, our situation...

But why do the fancy stuff when we haven't taken care of the fundamentals?

133 Why Is It So Difficult?

We often get to the point—when we're doing something that matters—where we ask *why is it so difficult?*

And the answer is: because we were so optimistic about our chances of success.

This isn't a negative. If we hadn't been optimistic we probably would never have started.

So let's rejoice in the difficulty and know that's why we're going to achieve whatever we want to achieve...

134 | I Wish It Was Harder

...and following on from yesterday's journal...

One of my Master Minders said, this month, that he wishes it was harder.

Surely that's crazy talk, right?

Not necessarily when you consider that:

1. However hard it is, he's *going to do the work needed.*

2. If it was harder, more of his competition would give up.

So next time we're tackling a difficult task, how about wishing it was harder?

135 Tiny Goals

When I started my YouTube channel, I set a tiny goal.

You see, if I said I wanted 10,000 subscribers I might get overwhelmed and put off starting.

But I didn't. And I won't.

Because my initial goal was 5 subscribers. Yes FIVE.

And once I have five, ten will be easy.

And if I can get ten, then fifty is reasonable.

And obviously if I can get fifty then 100 is entirely possible.

You get the idea.

Let's start with 5. The 10,000 or 100,000 or million will take care of themselves.

136 Weasel Guarantee

I saw a poster today from a broadband company offering a "minimum download speed, guaranteed".

The small-print was fascinating.

"Guarantee available for 64% of customers," and—more interestingly—*"measurements from 3rd party speed checkers will not be admitted."*

Now, don't get me wrong, guarantees are a great way to get business.

But let's not be weaselly about them... if we're going to make a grand claim, let's make sure it stands up to independent scrutiny.

This applies to everything. Let's be impeccable about our big promises.

137 The Joy of Being Wrong

Do you get annoyed with people who need to be 'right' all the time?

I used to.

And the reason I was annoyed was because I recognised that need in myself, and didn't like it.

Well, life has a habit of teaching us the lessons we need at exactly the time we need them, and boy has my ego taken a battering over the last few months.

Just yesterday, I had a problem with my car. I have a history of fixing my own car (I used to drive the kind of cars that garages would swear at when I booked them in), so rather than just go straight to the garage I had a little look myself.

Ok, it won't start. Let's try the battery. Let's try jump-starting. Let's try X, Y and Z.

After a whole host of tests, I figured it definitely wasn't the battery, and would be something I didn't want to fix myself, so I went to the garage.

"Have you tried a booster pack?" they asked? "No", I admitted.

They put the booster pack on, turned the key and the car started immediately.

"It's the battery."

Dammit.

There's a real joy in thinking we're so smart, thinking that we have all the answers, thinking that we're the bees knees, and having someone who actually knows what they're doing swipe that arrogance away in one swift blow.

(Or we can choose to get uptight about it. I choose to enjoy it!)

138 Write it in big!

Sometimes, in order to learn from our mistakes, mis-understandings and mis-assumptions, we need to 'write it in big'.

Here is a small selection of things I've 'written in big' over the last six months...

We all get to make it up, all of the time.

The challenges and struggles in the outer world are very often a reflection of the challenges and struggles in ourselves.

Feel the fear, and take a gentle step.

People know what to do, but they don't do what they know.

Be impeccable with your word.

What have you 'written in big'?

139 The Truth

The problem with truth is that there doesn't appear to be an objective form of it.

And while we're messing about figuring whether Donald Trump really said this or that, or what's going on with those secret 'elite' people we hear about, we're missing a major opportunity... and that's to figure out *our own* truth.

Let's just take a quick look at ourselves (in the mirror if necessary).

What are we putting off because we fear failure? Or maybe success?

What are we putting up with because we're busy pretending we're 'fine'?

What habits do we have that aren't helping us, but we don't want to even admit to ourselves that they're real?

What unpleasant actions are we complicit in because we pretend they're not going on?

Who are we, really? And will we let that person out into the world, and stand fearlessly in our own truth?

140 Owning Your Shadow

Continuing from yesterday's talk about the truth, one of the really inconvenient truths we don't want to deal with is our shadow.

This is the taboo stuff, the 'bad' stuff, the thoughts and feelings we have that we know society won't approve of.

So we push them down and pretend we're not having them.

The only problem with that is that like anything that's been compressed and squeezed, it takes a lot of energy to keep in its place, and if we take our attention off it for just a moment, it bursts back up to bite us on the bum.

I'm not suggesting we act out our darkest fantasies and desires, but we can at least acknowledge that they're there, and that they're ours.

And that's when they start to lose their power over us.

If you'd like to learn more, there's an excellent book called: *Owning Your Own Shadow*[15] *by Robert A. Johnson*. It's a quick read that gets you started nicely...

---

15. Owning Your Own Shadow, Robert A. Johnson, ISBN: 978-0062507549

141 Trust The Data

Sometimes you just have to trust the data.

I've been split-testing the sign-up form for one of my books. Three variants are nicely branded with nice colours.

The fourth has an ugly green button.

The fourth is also performing 328% better than the other three variants.

I don't like the ugly green button, but it works.

I guess sometimes we have to do the thing we don't like so much, because it works. This is probably true of more than we can imagine.

142 Fooled By Hollywood

Hollywood would have us believe that change and growth are easy. If we believed the movies, we'd believe that a quick three-week montage with an inspirational soundtrack will allow us to make any change we want in our lives.

Likewise, if we look at external results, we might be tempted to support that belief.

But it's not quite like that, is it?

The external results are just that, a result. It's not where the work is done. The work is done inside.

The results may come quickly, in a step-change, in an "overnight success" kind of way; but they only come because of a long-term commitment to do the *inner* work.

To apply our desired change with consistency and discipline over the necessary time; however long that is.

Let's apply consistency and discipline. The results will come on their own. When they're ready.

And then people will tell us how lucky we are to have an overnight success.

143 "Spirit" Day

Each week, Friday is my 'spirit' day.

I avoid taking on too many commitments, I avoid creating too much stuff, I avoid any tricky admin (hard spreadsheets, or calling HMRC for example!)

And I spend the day in mindfulness of my position in the world.

As I go about my business, I become acutely aware of whether I'm going where I want to go, whether I'm providing the value I want to provide, whether I'm living my life or going through the motions.

And I find it's a vitally important balancing tool that allows me to live and work with joy and gratitude.

I can recommend it.

And if you don't have time for such luxuries, you definitely need to do it!

144 The Best Bits

Those imperfections and flaws we have—the ones that we've spent countless energy on hiding and denying from ourselves and others—are our best bits.

They're the most fun, the most human, the most joyous.

They're what make us truly stand out from everyone else.

Let's celebrate them!

145 Seven Figures

Want to earn seven figures but can't? (Or reach any other kind of milestone or goal... this applies whatever it is you're trying to achieve...)

It's about the stories we tell ourselves (often being unaware that we're telling them).

Our inner voice and feelings may say "I'm not the kind of person who earns seven figures"

Or we may choose to programme a different story... "I'm definitely the kind of person to earn seven figures, I just haven't quite got it all figured out yet."

These two people are in exactly the same situation, but only one of them is likely to reach their goal.

146 Mopping Up

Few of us are tenacious enough to keep at it through thick and thin.

And so there are many who fall by the wayside.

Two incidents have happened this week—one in my life and one in one of my Master Minders'—where a gap has been left by someone who has given up.

Let's be the ones who mop up, and fill the void left by those who didn't see it through. Let's flow into the hollow and fill it up with our personal energy and uniqueness. Let's serve those who have been let down.

147   Dog Ends

I was following a chap through town today. He looked a little 'worse for wear', but in that 'still making an effort' way.

As we walked past the opticians, he stopped, bent down, picked up a discarded dog-end of a cigarette, examined it for its potential, dropped it and went on his way.

It's then that I realised...

We're all capable of seeing exactly what we want to see.

When we train our brain to look out for things, it'll spot them automatically and with no effort on our part.

So what will we choose to set our search parameters to? Dog-ends or opportunities? Problems or solutions? Need or abundance?

148 Abundance Blocks

Ever found yourself having an abundance block?

Could it be because you're asking the wrong question (as I did for an embarrassingly large number of years)...

What do I really need?

...is a valid and helpful question.

But what's the silent subtext? Are we asking:

What do I really need to survive? or What do I really need to thrive?

The difference is huge.

149 The Dragon

We all have a dragon guarding the door to our greatest wealth and prosperity.

But the problem with dragons is that they don't exist — they're invisible. And when we're faced with an invisible obstacle, all we have stopping us is our fear.

The key is to realise that we can see the dragon, or at least feel it. It lives in the subconscious realm, so we can become aware of—and make a difference to—our dragon only in our subconscious world... that's the world of our dreams and the world of our feelings.

And once we've identified and become aware of the dragon we can choose to defeat it or tame it. If it can guard our prosperity from us, it can do a great job of guarding it from other threats.

Will we take on the brave task of taming our dragon?

150 Systems

We're not robots. But if we don't have systems in place, we are missing out on one of the best mind-clarifyng tools known to man—or woman—kind.

Let's not keep all that information locked up and blocked... let's get the mundane stuff out, so our pure creative genius can shine through.

151 Five Things

I was reminded recently to write down, at the end of each day, five good things that have happened.

The benefit is twofold:

Firstly, we notice how much good stuff is going on in our lives; even on a "bad" day.

Secondly, we find ourselves taking more action, having more fun and living more life in order to have things to write down.

152 You are *not* a Commodity

I was working with a client the other day, and we got onto the subject of pricing. She explained that she falls in the 'industry norm' for her pricing, and sits on the low end of it due to relative lack of experience when she started up.

I wasn't buying that.

I know this person. She is outstanding. She brings massive value to any relationship due to her unique insight, talents and personality.

And the problem with falling into industry norms is that we're making the mistake of thinking we're a commodity.

She is not a commodity. I am not a commodity. And *you* are not a commodity.

Let's all recognise the unique values we bring to the table, and stop scrabbling around in the competitive world of "industry norms". Let's soar out of the norms, both with our proposition and our rewards.

The air is much clearer up here.

153 The Trust of our Inner Child

Our Inner Child is amazing. It is the source of all of our creativity and pure joy.

But as we grow up, we start to ignore its voice. "That's not grown-up" we say... "That's silly"... "Don't be so immature"... "Proper grown-ups don't do that"

And so our Inner Child stops talking to us. And stops trusting us. And starts kicking off at the slightest things.

When we realise we all have a scared six-year-old inside us, and we nurture that six-year-old, and we listen to it, and we do what we say we're going to do, it starts talking to us again. It gets comfortable in our company. And it allows us to, once again, experience that pure creativity and endless joy of life.

Let's build a strong, trusting and helpful relationship with our Inner Child.

154 Next Time Round

Remember... if we mess up this time, we'll take all those lessons into our next time round.

The next time round is always much easier.

(Apart from the new lessons we need to learn, naturally)

But the key point is that we can't have a 'next time round' if we don't get on with our 'this time round'.

155 Our Unique Value

Always remember that we struggle to see our own value. To us it's "normal" it's "just what we do".

Ask five close friends, today, what's unique about you; what you do differently than anyone else; what you do better than anyone else.

Listen and act on the responses.

156 The Big Issue with the Ego

We're all somewhat aware of when our ego takes over and hinders us in life, yes?

And do you know the biggest problem with that?

The problem is that the ego is *extremely* protective of itself, so we meet massive resistance whenever we try to do any work on it.

But that doesn't mean we should give up, it doesn't mean we shouldn't try.

It *can* be tamed. And then we can move forwards.

157 Change

It's unlikely that we'll change *them*. Or *it*.

So let's change *us*.

When *we* change, the world changes with us.

158 Hourly Billing

Are you still billing by the hour?

You know it makes no sense at all, right?

A supplier, billing by the hour, gets penalised for being good at what they do. If they provide their value efficiently and deliver quicker than expected, they get paid less.

And a client, being billed by the hour, gets penalised twice for shoddy work… if it takes their supplier a long time to pick their way through the work, the client gets it late *and* pays more.

It's nice to use the 'hourly rate' as an internal idea; to make sure we can earn what we want to earn in the hours given to us each day.

But let's never present an hourly rate to our clients, or we'll be ripping them, and us, off.

159 Boundaries

If we're ever upset at how others treat us, it's more about what going on inside us than what they're about.

There are three simple (but not necessarily easy) steps to take:

1. Decide on our boundaries, fearlessly.

2. Honour our own boundaries and live them.

3. See how others' treatment of us changes.

When we know our own boundaries—the important, non-negotiables of our lives—we will communicate them silently to the world. But we *do* have to know what they are.

160 What's the Hurry?

Something I regularly pick my clients and Master Minders up on is their tendency to place their happiness in the future, not now.

And Alan Watts—who I love for his no-nonsense approach to the world—had a fantastic way of putting it:

"If you hurry to get to the future, you always get a punishment for it. For example, instant coffee."

Let's be aware of the punishments we receive for hurrying.

161 Discipline

We sometimes rebel against discipline, don't we? Probably because we have these hang-ups about school and parents and having to do what we don't want to do.

But it's not *discipline* at fault. It's the actions we were expected to carry out; actions that we didn't see the point of.

And so, rather than rebel, let's use discipline to get where we want to be.

162   School

We go to school for, what, 14 years? And every day we are taught to lean on an external authority to:

1. Structure our days and time

2. Tell us how we should live our lives

3. Give us rewards for being 'good'

When we leave school, we leave physically, but forget to leave psychologically. This is great news, respectively, for:

Employers, politicians and those who want to control us

Glossy magazines and other companies who make money from our deepest insecurities

Providers of 'naughty but nice' treats such as fast food, cream cakes and cigarettes

It's not great news, however, for us.

Let's recognise the conditioning and 'leave school'. Let's look inside, rather than relying on an external authority.

163 If you think the whole world is insane...

If you think the whole world is insane... then you're right. We spoke yesterday about school and the conditioning it leaves us with.

The big problem in the world today is that there are much more effective ways we could work. There are better models for bringing value, earning, interacting and connecting.

But most of the population has a massive fear... the fear of what happens if they drop their dependence on the external authority.

They don't trust themselves enough to rely on their inner guidance.

And while that's the case, we'll collectively follow the external guidance of those who fight and scrabble egoically to the top.

This isn't a call to anarchy. Anarchy is a lack of authority.

This is a call to *inner* authority; doing the right thing because it's right, not because someone told us to do it.

164 "Self-Help" is a Rude Word

"Self-Help" is a rude word, and rightly so.

There are those who tell us to get up at 5am and all our dreams will come true. Except that they don't check our circadian rhythms, and what works for *us*. There are plenty of successful people I know who don't even get out of bed until 10am.

There are those who tell us that if we visualise our ideal future it will appear. It won't. We have to take the actions and do the work too. There is no magic pill.

There are those who tell us we're a broken mess and they can fix us. That is absolutely not true. We are *not* broken. We are exactly what we need to be right here, right now.

The main problem with 'self-help' is when it becomes "external help with no concept of what our 'self' needs".

True self-help is just us doing the *stuff* and acting on the insights to become our best selves.

Burnt Toast

Have you heard of 'burnt toast' syndrome?

That's where a parent is providing the breakfast for the family and a couple of the slices of toast get burnt.

"I'll have those", they say.

What they don't realise is that they're also giving a strong message to their subconscious... "I'm not good enough."

So let's not eat the burnt toast.

We can either share it out (but then we have to choose who gets it) or we can just put another couple of pieces in the toaster.

Let's not settle for burnt toast.

166 You Are Awesome

We often forget, so here's just another gentle reminder...

You are awesome! You are unique.

Your value doesn't come from what you have done or what you plan to do or how nice you are or, indeed, from any label that we might try to hang on you.

Your value comes from your unique mix of good, bad, genius, stupid, inspiration and confusion.

That's why you are awesome.

167 Carrying Tension

Here's something I do often... and it's probably my yoga practice—four months and counting—that has helped me to become aware of this...

As I'm walking along, I notice the tension I'm carrying in my hands, my arms, my shoulders, my neck and my core, and I consciously relax them all.

Become aware. Are you carrying unnecessary tension around with you?

Check yourself several times a day, the results are fascinating.

168 Travel and Freedom

I've seen reports recently that say Baby Boomers worked all their life and waited until retirement to travel. Generation X are balancing their work and life to get more freedom and travel. While Millennials are choosing freedom and travel before they even go into the world of work.

So what causes this difference?

All sorts of theories abound. But there's a very simple one...

Maybe *everyone* is currently seeking more freedom and travel. Right now. Regardless of their generation.

Sometimes we can look for complicated causes where a simple one will suffice.

False Average

Yesterday I talked about occasions where a simple solution will suffice. But it's not always the case.

I attended a networking meeting the other day, and they had a chat on their ideal avatar to invite along. They polled the room for how long each person had been in business... 18 years, 20 years, 6 months, 2 years, 1 year, 16 years...

Then they took the average which came out around 8 years.

The conclusion: *we're looking for someone who has been in business for around 8 years.*

Wrong.

Looking at the data (and I'm going to guess at the causes here), we have a bunch of businesses who are new and haven't yet built their sources of leads – so a room of people is a good place to be. And there are other long-established companies who use old-school networking as their main source of new business. The middle was all but missing.

So, let's think *accurately* rather than over-simplifying *or* over-complicating.

170 All These Roads

I always have a little smile when anyone complains about the price of their road tax.

I pay just £17 per month for mine. And I get to use *all of these roads!*

Just look at them. All over the country. Big roads, small roads, fast roads, slow roads, bridges, roundabouts, traffic lights... I get to use all of that for just £17 per month.

Even if I had a fancypants 4×4 and was paying £50 a month or more, it's still a massive bargain!

Let's look at our expenses realistically *and gratefully...*

171 Get Lost

It was my 'spirit day' on Friday, the day where I catch up with who I am and what the hell I'm doing on this big rock in space.

I didn't get lost, but I did go for a long walk in the countryside to take in nature, the weather, and some deep chat with some good people.

I can strongly recommend it. Once a month take a day to remember what life is really about.

If you want to, that is. If you don't, don't.

172 Re-Birth

Sometimes our life overwhelms us. We wonder how we can start again, be re-born, make a fresh beginning...

And it's quite simple. We can make that commitment at any time of any day. We don't need to wait.

We imagine that the movie of our "life so far" has just finished and the credits begin to roll.

And now, we can write the sequel. What does our sequel look like? How do we get out of the life situation we don't like? Where do we find the extra strength and courage? Where does our persistence come from when the challenges come up to face us?

What will we put in our sequel?

173 Set The Intent

When we want something we often try to *make* it happen.

But that's not how the universe works. We expend large amounts of energy trying to control everything around us, so we end up tired and still haven't made it happen.

The solution is to go with the flow... to set our intent, and then *let it* happen.

This is the powerful way to get where we want to be.

174 Niche

Who do we help best? *How* do we help best?

Then why are we still trying to please everyone? Why are we keeping our genius locked up in order to be mediocre?

Is it because we fear cutting off the things that don't serve us? Are we attached to redundant thoughts, beliefs and feelings?

Will we take the courageous move to stand for something and let our genius shine?

175 Declutter

We hear about decluttering our homes, but what about other aspects of our lives...

We can declutter our business, our hobbies, our time, our friends, our social media, our sources of information...

Everything can be decluttered and cut back to that which serves us (whether that's through beauty or utility)

176 No Guilt

When we make a decision, how often do we feel guilty about the option not taken?

About the people we've let down, or the opportunity lost, or other aspects of the 'cons' we weighed up.

Let's make a commitment, today, to make our decisions boldly with all the information we have at the time, and then *feel no guilt*.

177 Personal Power

It's very easy to ask ourselves if changing some aspect of our life would make us better, more complete, more whole... but we've got it slightly wrong...

Examples: Would I get more clients if I drove a fancier car? Would I get a date if I lost a bit of weight? Would people take me more seriously if I wore smarter clothes?

The answer isn't to get the fancy car, lose the weight or get the smarter clothes; the answer is to remove the link between the problem and the perceived solution.

We may get more clients if we stop feeling bad about the car we have. We might get the date if we are confident about our weight, whatever it is. We might get taken more seriously if we didn't blame our clothes.

Let's be aware of the 'justification' lies we're telling ourselves, and remember that we have immense personal power whatever our life situation.

178 Because Everyone Else Does It

I was bumbling unconsciously into an action today, and suddenly wondered why I was about to do it the way I was about to do it...

"Because everybody does it that way", was my first response.

No no no. That's not a good enough reason.

I thought for a moment longer...

"Because it serves my best interests to do it that way."

Yes. That's a good enough reason.

179 Colours

I watched a very interesting Q&A session on YouTube the other day, and one of the simple, but powerful things that came out of it was this:

Don't take colours for granted.

Because they're all around us all the time, we fail to notice what a beautiful, vibrant, colourful world we live in.

What other ever-present things are we taking for granted? Customers? Family? Friends? Flavours? Time? What else?

180 If No-One Else Ever Saw It

We're all agreed that doing things just to please others is not so helpful, right?

So what about that fancy car? Do we want it because it's comfortable or quick or stylish? Or do we want it because we think it'll impress others?

Here's a test that one of my Master Minders introduced us to earlier this week...

If you knew that no-one else would ever see the thing you're about to buy, would you still buy it?

If the answer's yes, it's a good bet you're doing it for your own reasons.

181 If Everyone Knew...

The converse to yesterdays question is a good moral guide.

If you knew that everyone would find out about what you're about to do, would you still do it?

If the answer is yes, there's a good chance that you either don't give a cr#p about what people think (which isn't so bad in itself), or that your proposed activity is probably not so morally reprehensible!

182 Criticism

I met a chap the other day who has nine kids and is homeschooling them.

After a brief chat I saluted him for his vision, courage, and worldview (naturally adding that I knew he didn't need external validation).

He said that he does come against quite a lot of, shall we say, 'opinion' about his choices, perhaps bordering on criticism.

The problem with criticising others for their choices is that we're forgetting that *they're not us*. We're projecting *our* hopes, dreams, fears and desires onto them. And that's never helpful.

So let's celebrate and revel in the diverse life-choices of others. Who knows, we might learn something from them!

183 Guilt and Shame

Guilt says "I made a mistake"

Shame says "I *am* a mistake"

Let's endeavour to attach ourselves to neither of these damaging feelings. Let's, instead, love ourselves for who we are, right now, with what we have, and where we are in our life situation.

184 When walking, Walk

We so often fail to enjoy what we're doing because we're not *present*.

We can't focus on task X, because we're worried that we messed up task Y yesterday, or will mess up task Z tomorrow.

It's all summed up in the Zen proverb:

"When walking, walk. When eating, eat."

Let's focus on task X, whether it's work or play, whether it's highly enjoyable or a 'chore'.

185 The Collective Consciousness

The collective consciousness is raising.

What does that mean? It means that people are getting smarter; they're getting better at sniffing out the BS.

The lies have always been in politics, but now they're being recognised for what they are. The gurus are being 'found out' – their expertise doesn't work for everyone, and most people who pay for their help end up in the same place, but significantly poorer.

Marketers are getting more and more desperate, more competitive.

And we can join them if we like.

Or we can focus on truth and value – telling the truth, and providing genuine value.

We can adopt tactics, or we can just get on with doing an amazing job.

186 Waiting for Permission

I've seen a few clients this week who are all *waiting for permission* in some way.

We all do it. We think we're not qualified to do what we want to do; we think people won't take us seriously; we think people will question our credentials...

But when it comes down to it, the only person who is going to give us permission is *ourselves*.

So let's do it right now. Let's give ourselves permission to be the person we want to be.

187 Neutrality

Neutrality is such a powerful place to come from.

We no longer take failure or rejection personally. If it happens, it happens.

On the flipside, that means we can no longer take *success* personally. Again, if it happens, it happens.

Let's do the work we need to do, with our best intention, and detach ourselves from the outcomes. The ones that are meant to happen will happen.

188 Hustle Revisited

There's a lot of talk about 'hustle'; about working long hours, doing lots of stuff, using mind hacks to get the best productivity and employing all sorts of tactics to sell and get what we want.

And I'm sure it works for some people (though it just sounds exhausting to me).

So let's be aware that there is another way; a way that's worked for me and plenty of my clients...

And that is to *raise our energy, and respond to what shows up in the world.*

The hardest part of this method is boldly and truthfully working on ourselves. The easiest part is *everything else.*

No force. No angst. No fear. Just a peaceful 'show up, pay attention and respond' attitude.

If the 'hustle' route doesn't work for you, why not try out the 'energetic response' route?

189 Anger

A quick example to demonstrate yesterday's point about raising our energy...

If I'd written that blog a week ago, I would have said "Hustle is all bullsh#t. It's rubbish. It doesn't work."

But over the course of the last week I've recognised and released a lot of latent anger – that stuff that's just sitting around since the beginning of time (or since my formative years at least).

This is what 'raising our energy' is about. It's about being with, and releasing, our imprinted emotions—shame, guilt, anger, pride, grief to name a few—and allowing our personal power to shine.

The result is that hustle no longer bugs me. Those who feel the need to hustle are welcome to it. It's certainly one route to 'success' (whatever that means).

But it's not for me, and it's probably not for a lot of people.

And I still stand by my statement that it must be *exhausting!*

190 Meditation

What's meditation all about, then?

Sitting around doing nothing? Surely that doesn't get anything useful done.

Correct. It doesn't.

What it does do is acts as a 'gym for the mind'. We don't achieve *while* we're meditating, but we meditate to practice bringing present moment awareness to everything we do.

And *then* we get the useful stuff done. In abundance.

191 The Secret to Success

The secret to success is recognising that we are already successful *right now.*

We often put our success at some mystical point in the future that we can't quite reach.

We have to realise that the point in the future never comes, we must recognise the success that we have right now, where we are and with what we have.

192 Tough

Ever noticed that someone who makes a point of looking tough isn't so tough after all?

Someone who's genuinely tough doesn't have to make a show of it to convince others (or themselves).

The same is true of everything. Are we making too much effort to convince ourselves of something we're insecure about?

193 Effort

Sometimes we fail to finish things and, indeed, make them extra complicated just so we *can't* finish them.

And sometimes that's because we believe that our worth is in the *effort we're expending,* not the results we get.

Let's be mindful of this, and be happy with providing the 'easy' solution. It doesn't make it worth anything less.

194 What Is An Expert?

Sometimes we hold back from sharing our gift because we don't think we're enough of an expert.

But when we *do* share our gift—even the obvious stuff—we realise how *little* of it most people know.

Just because it's obvious and easy for us doesn't mean anyone else finds it obvious or easy.

Bewildering?

Sometimes I think the world gets more bewildering by the day.

But then I realise that the past was just as bewildering. We didn't know about hygiene and germs, we couldn't travel without being robbed by bandits or highwaymen, we (for the most part) had to farm land that belonged to someone else and pay for the privilege of surviving. (Ok... that last one still holds somewhat).

As we learn more, we learn how much we don't know. And we create new ways to be bewildered.

So let's not pretend it *was* better, or *will be* better. Let's get comfortable here, today, and *embrace* the bewilderment.

196 Truth

Ever struggled to get to the truth of a matter?

The problem is that we think there's one objective truth, when really there isn't.

Truth is entirely based on context, and someone else may have a different opinion than ourselves which is equally valid and 'true'.

So let's find out *our own* truth. And live it daily. And speak it fearlessly.

197 When?

When the question changes from 'if...' to 'when?', there's often only one reasonable answer...

And that answer is *'now'*.

198 Be Here, Now

Ever get that feeling that when you're going about your business you're not present? Your mind is on home, feeling guilty about the things you're missing out on.

And when you're at home, your mind is on your work. You then feel guilty that you're not giving your loved ones the time and attention that they deserve.

The solution is to *be* wherever you are. Be there fully, and engage with what's happening around you.

Let's not spend our lives always being 'somewhere else'.

199 Notifications

Have you noticed how many times we're interrupted each day by notifications?

Each interruption takes vital value out of our lives. We lose our train of thought, our concentration span is trained to shrink, our attention is always at the beckon call of others.

So let's disable our notifications, and check on things only when we *want* to check. Let's take back charge of our attention.

200 Remember to Breathe

Sometimes, just a single breath is all it takes to re-centre ourselves... not a dramatic "look at me, huff puff" breath, but a calm pause.

During that breath we allow ourselves to feel what we're *really* feeling. We allow ourselves to think what we're *really* thinking. No judgement, no criticism of ourselves, we just *be* for a moment.

And then we can continue with what we were doing, but with a new energy.

201 What is a Life Hack you think Everybody Should Know?

I was asked this a while ago, and if you're a regular reader you'll probably know my answer...

Ten minutes' silence at the start and end of every day.

Even if you can only make it five minutes, or even 30 seconds, taking that short time sitting in silence with no agenda, no thoughts, no plans, nowhere to be, nothing to do, can have a huge impact on your life.

The best ideas come to us in a tiny whisper, and being still and quiet for long enough allows us to hear our inner guidance.

202 Misconceptions about Minimalism

When you hear the word 'Minimalism', what do you think about? For many, it means pure white, spotless rooms; it means vegan diets; it means all-white or -black clothing; it means throwing out all of our worldly belongings and living with a single cup, bowl and spoon. But that's a misconception based on some of the more 'extreme' minimalists.

We can all introduce minimalism into our lives. The basic premise is to keep only what is valuable. And we get to choose what is valuable to us.

Minimalism doesn't tell us to throw everything out. It invites us to figure out if all of our clutter—all the things we're holding on to—are genuinely bringing joy into our lives (either through beauty or utility)

And it invites us to let those items that aren't valuable go somewhere that they will be more helpful, more useful, more loved.

So let's not get hung up on dogma, let's have a look at the possessions we have that annoy us the most and consider if they may be better placed in someone else's custody.

203 Saying "No"

It's something we fear to do; we think we'll turn opportunities away.

But sometimes that's exactly what we want to do – turn down the bad, mediocre, or sometimes even 'good' opportunities to leave room for the 'great' ones.

Sometimes we say lots of "yesses" to expand outwards and find what's a good direction to go, we meet lots of people and come up with lots of ideas, and encounter lots of opportunities.

But there also comes the time to focus – to start saying "no" to things so we can really put our efforts into the things we know (or have a good inkling) will work.

204 Move In The Same Direction

I went to a dance class yesterday. I'm not sure what came over me to sign up for it, but I have to say it's the most fun I've had on a Saturday morning for a while.

The golden rules I quickly learnt were:

1. Enjoy every moment.

2. If you can'd do the arms, just do the feet.

3. If you can't do the feet, at least move in the same direction as everyone else.

4. Enjoy every moment.

This is a lesson with wider implications, don't you think?

205 Are You Busy?

People continue to ask me if I'm busy, as if "yes" is the right answer.

It's my full-time job to *not* be busy. It allows me to be balanced, calm and on top form for the work I do with my clients.

And I believe everyone can benefit by being less busy. You see, it's in those less busy moments—the ones where we get to pause and breathe—that our inner guidance speaks to us and lets us know what we really want out of life.

But we also fear that voice... we fear what we'll meet when we take a moment away from our to-do list.

Are you busy? Is it because you're being productive or because you don't want to hear your own inner voice?

When We Label Emotions

If you study Zen for any amount of time you discover that much of our suffering comes from labelling things... "I am a bad person" or "That is wrong".

And we seem addicted to labelling our emotions. A feeling comes up in our body and we label it immediately as *fear* or *anger* or *excitement*.

What we don't realise is that emotions can't be labelled. They are merely flows of energy within our body. What we call *fear* might actually be *impending awesomeness*. What we call *anger* might be a *call to action*.

It's the stories we tell ourselves about our emotions that cause many of our problems.

So let's just feel the emotions without judging, labelling or thinking about them. Let's just allow the energy to move around... let's follow it with our awareness.

And let's drop the stories. Because then we can act in true authenticity instead of constantly suppressing, numbing and 'coping with' the emotions that we label as *bad*.

207 When I Fall

All learning comes from failing and falling.

When everything is going well, we learn nothing.

So let's allow ourselves to fall over more often (figuratively speaking, I'm not talking about overdoing the 'pop' on our next night out!)

Let's *allow* ourselves to fail. Because that's when we learn and grow.

208 Life, The Adventure

Life is truly an adventure...

No one knows how long it will be, no one knows who and what they'll encounter along the way and no one knows what the ultimate prize is.

We can only form a band of companions and face the challenges, celebrate the successes and enjoy the journey.

—

Until next year's Anthology...

Stay awesome, love unconditionally, and always remember to breathe...

Resources

About The Author

Stuart Carter believes that everyone is entitled to Simplicity, Clarity and Freedom in their lives and works with one-to-one clients as well as producing his journal, books, videos and podcasts for a diverse audience.

His one-to-one clients are high-performance women who want to attain and maintain success and happiness in their business and personal lives.

He also created **TheAscendingMan.com** for guys who are navigating their spiritual awakening; a process that Stuart found both bewlidering and massively rewarding in the summer of 2017.

In late 2017 he co-founded, along with fellow coach Tracy Prentice, **The Enlightened Entrepreneur**, which is a movement for the more spiritual curious business owner and self-employed. You can learn more at:

www.theEnlightenedEntrepreneur.uk

The overriding theme all of these ventures is very much in line with what you have read in this Anthology; to *focus on what's important and trust your inner guidance* – a way of life that is extremely simple, but not necessarily *easy*.

Keep In Touch...

If you have found these journals helpful you can subscribe to his "Journals to your Inbox" at:

daily.stuartcarter.co.uk

And you can support Stuart's journal on Patreon:

www.patreon.com/stuartcarter

If you'd like to get in touch to discuss any aspect of Stuart's work, enquire about having him speak at your event, or find out about working with him as a one-to-one client, please get in touch by leaving a message or—better—by sending an email:

01509 833 058 | stuart@stuartcarter.co.uk

Bibliography

The Millionaire Masterplan
Roger James Hamilton *(ISBN: 978-1455583997)*

The Power of Now
Eckhart Tolle *(ISBN: 978-0340733509)*

Rich Dad Poor Dad
Robert Kiyosaki *(ISBN: 978-1612680194)*

Wink
Roger James Hamilton*(ISBN: 978-9810583828)*

Zero Resistance Selling
Maxwell Maltz *(ISBN: 978-0735200395)*

The Rules of Life
Richard Templar *(ISBN: 978-1292085609)*

How To Get Rich
Felix Dennis *(ISBN: 978-0091921668)*

Secrets of the Millionaire Mind
T. Harv Eker *(ISBN: 978-0749927899)*

Evil By Design
Chris Nodder *(ISBN: 978-1118422144)*

Hooked: How To Build Habit-Forming Products
Nir Eyal *(ISBN: 978-0241184837)*

Eat That Frog!
Brian Tracy *(ISBN: 978-1444765427)*

Owning Your Own Shadow : Understanding the Dark Side of the Psyche
Robert A. Johnson *(ISBN: 978-0062507549)*

Also Available

The 80/20 Blueprint : The concise guide to working less and achieving more.
ISBN: 978-1530964635

The book that's purposefully short.

The 80/20 Blueprint is the quickest way for the ambitious business owner to start implementing the natural law of 80/20 in their business and life, leading to more results for less effort and gaining the freedom they dreamed of when they started their business in the first place.

Discover Your 80/20 Vision : How to know what's important. And what to do about it.
ISBN: 978-1530958733

For the first time, we join the dots on what's been missing all this time. The magic 'spark' that will join your hopes and dreams to your day-to-day business and life.

It's not just about having your cake and eating it, it's about dreaming up your ideal cake and taking the most efficient route to holding it in your hands!

Available now from Amazon and other book sellers.

23241136R00148

Printed in Poland
by Amazon Fulfillment
Poland Sp. z o.o., Wrocław